Brad Miser

Sams **Teach Yourself**

Mac OS® X Lion™

in **10 Minutes**

800 East 96th Street, Indianapolis, Indiana 46240

Sams Teach Yourself Mac OS® X Lion™ in 10 Minutes

Copyright © 2012 by Pearson Education, Inc.

International Standard Book Number-10: 0-672-33570-0

International Standard Book Number-13: 978-0-672-33570-9

Library of Congress Cataloging-in-Publication data is on file.

Trademarks

All terms mentioned in this book that are known to be trademarks or service marks have been appropriately capitalized. Pearson cannot attest to the accuracy of this information. Use of a term in this book should not be regarded as affecting the validity of any trademark or service mark.

Warning and Disclaimer

Bulk Sales

Pearson offers excellent discounts on this book when ordered in quantity for bulk purchases or special sales. For more information, please contact

U.S. Corporate and Government Sales
1-800-382-3419
corpsales@pearsontechgroup.com

For sales outside of the U.S., please contact

International Sales
international@pearsoned.com

Editor In Chief
Greg Wiegand

Aquisitions Editor
Laura Norman

Development Editor
Charlotte Kughen, The Wordsmithery LLC

Technical Editor
Paul Sihvonen-Binder

Managing Editor
Sandra Schroeder

Project Editor
Mandie Frank

Copy Editor
Megan Wade

Indexer
Heather McNeill

Proofreader
Debbie Williams

Production
Mark Shirar

Designer
Gary Adair

Contents

About the Author

Brad Miser has written extensively about technology, with his favorite topics being Apple's amazing Macintosh computers, iPods, and iPhones. Books Brad has written include: *Sams Teach Yourself iTunes 10 in 10 Minutes*; *My iPod touch,* Second Edition; *My iPhone,* Fourth Edition; *Easy iLife '09*; *Special Edition Using Mac OS X Leopard*; *Absolute Beginner's Guide to Homeschooling*; *Teach Yourself Visually MacBook,* Third Edition; and *MacBook Pro Portable Genius,* Third Edition. He has also been an author, development editor, or technical editor on more than 50 other titles.

Brad is or has been a sales support specialist, the director of product and customer services, and the manager of education and support services for several software development companies. Previously, he was the lead proposal specialist for an aircraft engine manufacturer, a development editor for a computer book publisher, and a civilian aviation test officer/engineer for the U.S. Army. Brad holds a Bachelor of Science degree in mechanical engineering from California Polytechnic State University at San Luis Obispo and has received advanced education in maintainability engineering, business, and other topics.

Originally from California, Brad now lives in Brownsburg, Indiana, with his wife Amy; their three daughters, Jill, Emily, and Grace; a rabbit; and a sometimes-inside cat.

Brad would love to hear about your experiences with this book (the good, the bad, and the ugly). You can write to him at bradmiser@me.com.

Dedication

To those who have given the last full measure of devotion so the rest of us can be free.

Acknowledgments

A special thanks to Laura Norman, Acquisitions Editor extraordinaire, for involving me in this project. I appreciate the efforts of Charlotte Kughen, Development Editor, for ensuring the content of this book is meaningful and does allow you to learn Mac OS X Lion in 10 minutes. Thanks to Paul Sihvonen-Binder, the Technical Editor who made sure this book is accurate and "tells it like it is." Megan Wade deservers special mention for transforming my gibberish into readable text. And Sandra Schroeder and Mandie Frank deserve kudos for the difficult task of coordinating all the many pieces, people, and processes that are required to make a book happen. Last, but certainly not least, to the rest of the important folks on the team, including Heather McNeill, Cindy Teeters, Gary Adair, Mark Shirar, and the rest of the top-notch Sams staff, I offer a sincere thank you for all of your excellent work on this project.

We Want to Hear from You

As the reader of this book, you are our most important critic and commentator. We value your opinion and want to know what we're doing right, what we could do better, what areas you'd like to see us publish in, and any other words of wisdom you're willing to pass our way.

You can email or write me directly to let me know what you did or didn't like about this book—as well as what we can do to make our books stronger.

Please note that I cannot help you with technical problems related to the topic of this book, and that due to the high volume of mail I receive, I might not be able to reply to every message.

When you write, please be sure to include this book's title and author, as well as your name and contact information. I will carefully review your comments and share them with the author and editors who worked on the book.

Email: consumer@samspublishing.com

Mail: Greg Wiegand
          Editor In Chief
          Sams Publishing
          800 East 96th Street
          Indianapolis, IN 46240 USA

Introduction

Mac OS X, now in the Lion release (version 10.7 for those of you who aren't crazy about big cats), is the software that runs all Macintosh computers from the top-of-the-line Power Mac to the extremely popular MacBook laptops. This software provides the desktop from which all your activities start, enables you to configure and personalize your Mac, and controls all the applications and the many processes that are required to make your Mac do all the great things it can do. Along with the operating system itself, Mac OS X Lion includes many applications that you can use to surf the Web, email, chat (text, audio, and video), keep track of your time and contacts, and much more. Learning how to use Mac OS X Lion enables you to get the most fun and productivity from your Mac; this book helps you tame this lion (sorry, I had to make a bad pun with this at some point so I figured I'd get it out of the way early).

About This Book

Similar to the other books in the *Sams Teach Yourself in 10 Minutes* series, the purpose of this book is to enable you to learn how to use Mac OS X Lion quickly and easily; hopefully, you'll even enjoy yourself along the way! This book is composed of a series of lessons. Each lesson covers a specific aspect of using Mac OS X Lion. For example, Lesson 4, "Touring Lion's Applications," teaches you how to work with applications, and Lesson 8, "Working with Mice, Trackpads, and Keyboards," shows you how to use all sorts of input devices.

The lessons generally build on each other starting with the more fundamental topics covered in the earlier lessons and moving toward more advanced topics in the later lessons. In general, if you work from the front of the book toward the back, your Mac OS X Lion education will progress smoothly (of course, if a specific topic is of interest to you, you can jump ahead to get there first).

The lessons include both information and explanations along with step-by-step tasks. You'll get more out of the lessons if you perform the steps as you read the lessons. Figures are included to show you what key steps look like on your computer's screen.

Who This Book Is For

This book is for anyone who wants to get the most out of Mac OS X Lion; Mac OS X Lion is widely recognized as the most intuitive and easy-to-use operating system, but even so, you'll learn much faster with this guide to help you. If you've never used Mac OS X Lion, this book can get you started and help you move toward becoming a Mac OS X Lion guru. If you've dabbled with Mac OS X Lion, this book helps you go beyond basic tasks to be able to use all of Mac OS X Lion's amazing functionality. If you've spent a fair amount of time using Mac OS X Lion, this book provides lessons to round out your Mac OS X Lion expertise.

What Do I Need to Use This Book?

The only technical requirement to be able to use this book is a computer with Mac OS X Lion installed on it. Much of Mac OS X Lion's functionality requires an Internet connection, so you'll have a much better experience if you can connect your computer to the Net (you'll learn how to do this, too).

In addition to the basic technical requirements, you need a sense of adventure and curiosity to explore all this book offers you. Mac OS X Lion is fun to use and, with this guide to help you, it should be fun to learn as well.

Conventions Used in This Book

Whenever you need to click a particular button or link or make a menu selection, you see the name of that item in **bold**, such as "Click the **Save** button to save your document." You'll also find three special elements (Notes, Tips, and Cautions) throughout the book.

NOTE: A note provides information that adds to the knowledge you gain through each lesson's text and figures.

TIP: Tips offer alternative ways to do something, such as keyboard shortcuts, or point out additional features.

CAUTION: You won't find many of these in this book, but when you do come across one, you should carefully read it to avoid problems or situations that could cause you grief, time, or money.

LESSON 1

Getting Started with Mac OS X Lion

In this lesson, you learn how to get started using a Mac running Mac OS X Lion.

Touring the Lion Desktop

The Macintosh Operating System, Lion (10.7) version, or Mac OS X Lion for short, is one of the most powerful and easy-to-use computer operating systems. After you've spent some time on its desktop, which is what you see on your Mac's screen, you'll soon feel right at home here.

The desktop displays content through windows that, just like windows in the real world, enable you to see things. What you see depends on the context in which you are working. When you are running an application, you see the content you are creating or editing in that application, such as text and graphics in a word processing document, or content that you are using, such as a webpage, music, or video.

When you are on the desktop, you see a variety of objects, which are shown in Figure 1.1 and described in the following sections. You learn how to use what is on your desktop throughout the rest of this book. In this lesson, focus on getting an overview of what you see and understanding the key concepts so you become comfortable with the contents of your desktop. Becoming comfortable with what you see on the desktop is the first step in learning how to use a Mac running Mac OS X Lion.

Starting Up and Logging In

Of course, to get started with your Mac, you turn it on. It's likely you've already done this. The first time you start your Mac, Mac OS X Lion's

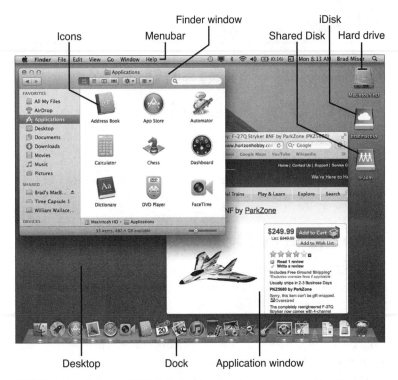

FIGURE 1.1 The Mac OS X Lion desktop is where you work with documents, view webpages, and much more.

Assistant walks you through the basic configuration of your Mac. The
Assistant appears only the first time you power a Mac up.

To start your Mac, you press the Power key, which is a round button with a
circle and vertical line running through it. The location of this button
depends on the specific kind of Mac computer you are using. For example,
if you are working with a MacBook or MacBook Pro, this button is located
on the upper-right corner of the keyboard. When you press this button, the
Mac powers on and loads the software it needs to run, which is Mac OS X
Lion. This software controls everything that happens on your Mac.

Mac OS X is a multiuser system, meaning that to use it, you need to have
a user account. Like other user accounts, a Mac OS X user account has an

account name and a password. You provide these credentials to log in to Mac OS X so you can access your specific resources on the computer.

When you work through the assistant the first time you start your Mac, you create a user account including the account name and password. However, by default, the assistant sets automatic login, which means the account information is entered for you automatically each time you start your computer, so you don't have to enter it yourself. In Lesson 9, "Configuring and Managing User Accounts," you learn how to turn off automatic login and work with user accounts.

When automatic login is disabled and you start up your Mac, you must log in to a user account. Depending on your Mac's configuration, you see either a list of user accounts or empty username and password fields. You use one or the other of these screens to log in to your Mac so you can start using it.

If you see a screen similar to Figure 1.2, perform the following steps to log in:

1. Point to the user account you want to use. (If you don't understand pointing and clicking, skip these steps for now and read this entire lesson; then come back to these steps.)

2. Click the icon for the user account you want to use. You are prompted to enter the associated password.

3. Type the password for the user account you clicked in step 2.

4. Press the Return key. If you provided the correct password for the user account you selected, you move onto your desktop and your Mac is ready to use. If you didn't provide the correct password, the screen "shivers" and you need to enter it again.

If you see the screen shown in Figure 1.3, perform the following steps instead:

1. Click in the top box. (If you don't understand pointing and clicking, skip these steps for now and read this entire lesson; then come back to these steps.)

2. Type the username for the account you want to use.

FIGURE 1.2   On this version of the Login window, you see an icon for each user account on your Mac.

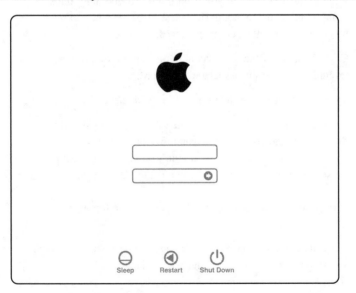

FIGURE 1.3   On this version of the Login window, you enter a username and password to log in.

3. Press the Tab key. You move into the Password field.

4. Type the password for the username you typed in step 2.

5. Press the Return key. If you provided a valid username and password, you move onto your desktop and your Mac is ready to use. If you didn't provide the correct information, the screen "shivers" and you need to enter it again.

Pointing, Clicking, Dragging, and Scrolling

Mac OS X Lion uses a graphical interface; this means that you interact with graphical objects on the screen, such as icons, windows, and so on. Before you interact with something, you must tell Mac OS X with which object you want to interact. You do this by pointing to the object with which you want to work. The pointer that appears on the screen tells Mac OS X where your focus is, and it is how you tell the software what you want to take action on. You do this by moving the pointer; when you are working on the desktop, the pointer is an arrow. In other situations, it can become other icons, but after you've used the arrow pointer, you can use any of them.

To move the pointer around the screen, you can use a mouse or trackpad (there are other options, but these are the two that are used by the vast majority of Mac users).

When you move a mouse on your physical desktop, the pointer moves with it. To move up the screen, push the mouse away from you; to move it down the screen, pull the mouse toward you. Moving the mouse to the left or right moves the pointer to the left or right.

To point with a trackpad, move a finger toward the "top" of the trackpad (toward the screen) to move the pointer up the screen; moving your finger toward you moves the pointer down the screen. Moving your finger to the left or right causes the pointer to move to the left or right.

NOTE: **Pointing Speeds**

In Lesson 5, "Personalizing Lion," you learn how to control how far the pointer moves in relation to moving the mouse or your fingers on a trackpad. As you get more comfortable, you'll probably want the pointer to move faster so you can get around the desktop more quickly.

Pointing to an object doesn't tell the Mac OS when you are ready to take action; this is where clicking comes in. When you click on an object, you tell the OS that you've reached the object in which you are interested; this is also called *selecting* an object. How you click depends on the specific mouse or trackpad you are using. If you are using a Magic Mouse, you click by pressing down on the top of the mouse once until it "clicks." Other types of mice might have a button you click instead. If you are using a trackpad, you press it once or tap it once to click. When you click on (select) an object, it usually becomes highlighted in some way, such as turning dark gray, which is your visual confirmation that you have selected it.

A double-click opens an object. As you probably can guess, you double-click by pressing the top of the mouse twice in relatively rapid fashion; on a trackpad, you press or tap twice. After the second click, your Mac opens the object on which you clicked. This could be an application, in which case it starts running; a folder, in which case it opens and you see its contents; a document, which then opens in a window; a menu, which opens to show you the commands you can perform; and so on.

Yet another kind of click is the secondary click. This typically opens a contextual menu from which you can choose commands to perform on the object you pointed to before you performed the secondary click. Although you can use your Mac just fine without ever performing a secondary click, using this will make using a Mac much faster because it reduces the number of mouse motions and key presses. How you can perform a secondary click depends on how the device you are using is configured (you learn how to configure a mouse and trackpad in Lesson 5), but you can always perform a second click by holding the Control key down and clicking the mouse or trackpad button. A menu appears and you can choose a command; what is on this menu depends on the object on which you performed the secondary click.

NOTE: **Left- and Right-Clicks**

Some mice have buttons you click. The left button is usually a single-click, while the right button is a secondary click. Because of this, you will often hear the term *right-click* used instead of the more formal term *secondary click*.

Another important Mac skill is dragging. This is how you move or copy objects. To drag something, you single-click on it so it becomes highlighted but don't release your click. If you are using a mouse, keep pressing down on the top of the mouse; if you are using a trackpad, don't lift your finger. The object on which you clicked remains selected and is "attached" to the pointer; as you move the pointer, so moves the object. When you have reached your destination, release the mouse or lift your finger and the object is "dropped" in its new location. This action is often referred to as *drag and drop*.

NOTE: **Trackpad Dragging**

With a trackpad, you can drag using a gesture, which is touching three fingers to the trackpad when you are pointing to the object you want to move. As you move your fingers, the object moves on the screen. To release it, lift your fingers off the trackpad. You learn how to set this preference in Lesson 5.

As you work in windows (which you'll get to in the next section), you need to scroll to see all the contents in a window. Scrolling happens in all four directions (up, down, left, and right). There are several ways to scroll.

One is to drag the scrollbars in the direction you want to scroll. Another is to move two fingers on a trackpad or on the top of a Magic Mouse to move the content being displayed around so you can see all of it.

Understanding Windows

Anything you view on your Mac is looked at through a window. There are many types of windows, including windows for applications, documents, folders, and so on. Fortunately, even though there are many types of windows, they have certain elements that are consistent no matter what type of window you are working with. (The details of using windows are provided in Lesson 2, "Working on the Lion Desktop"). Figure 1.4 shows the elements of a Finder window, and Figure 1.5 shows an application window.

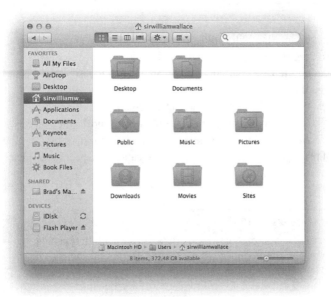

FIGURE 1.4   You use Finder windows constantly as you use your Mac because they are usually the starting point for tasks.

FIGURE 1.5   This example of a window shows a webpage; notice it has some of the same elements as the Finder window in Figure 1.4.

The following is an overview of elements that are common to almost all windows:

▶ **Close button**. The red button in the upper-left corner of a window is the Close button. The window you were viewing closes; if you were working with a document that has unsaved changes, you are prompted to save your changes before the window closes. In other situations, the window just disappears from the desktop.

▶ **Minimize button**. Just to the right of the Close button is the **yel-**low Minimize button. When you click this, the window remains open but "shrinks" and moves onto the Dock. You can return to the window by clicking its icon.

▶ **Zoom button**. The green Zoom button either causes windows to open to the size needed to view all the contents of the window or causes the window to be as large as possible. Clicking it again returns the window to its previous size.

▶ **Title**. The text in the center of the top of the window is the name of whatever you are viewing. For example, when you are viewing a webpage, this is the name of the page. When you are viewing a document, it is the document's filename. When you are viewing a Finder window, this is the name of the folder whose content you are viewing.

▶ **Toolbar**. Most windows have a toolbar at the top. This toolbar contains icons on which you can click to perform actions related to the content of the window.

▶ **Resize handles**. Although the resize handles are not a visible feature, you can drag the corners or any side of a window to resize it. To do this, point to the corner or side of the window you want to resize. When the arrow pointer becomes a diagonal line with an arrow on each end, you can resize the window. Drag the handle until the window is the shape and size you want it to be. When you release the drag, the window retains its new size.

▶ **Scrollbars**. When a window has more content than can be displayed, you can scroll around within it. As you scroll, scrollbars might appear to indicate your relative position in the window if you have set the preference for them to be visible (see Figure 1.6); you can also drag on these bars to move around inside a window. Scrollbars appear along the right edge of the window for vertical scrolling or along the bottom side of a window for horizontal scrolling. A Mac OS X setting determines how and when scrollbars appear; by default, they appear automatically based on the type of input device you are using (such as a mouse or trackpad). For example, when you drag two fingers on a trackpad to scroll, the scrollbar appears while you are dragging. When you lift your fingers, it disappears again.

Scrollbar

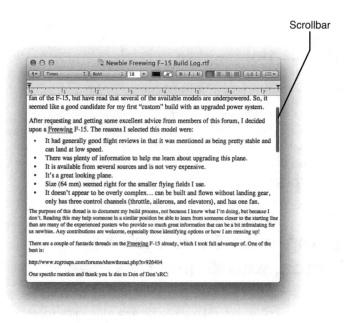

FIGURE 1.6   Scrollbars indicate your relative position within a window.

Understanding Applications, Files, and Folders

Much of what you do on your Mac involves applications, files, and folders.

An *application* is a collection of computer code that translates commands you select and input you make into information, actions, and everything else that happens on your Mac. You use a lot of applications as you work with your Mac. In Lesson 3, "Installing, Using, and Managing Applications," you learn how to install and manage applications. Mac OS X Lion includes a number of applications by default; you learn about these in Lesson 4, "Touring Lion's Applications." The application that runs your desktop is the Finder, so you use the Finder quite a lot.

A file is a container for data. Files can contain many kinds of data. For example, some files are documents, such as text documents you create with a word processor. Files can also be images, songs, movies, and other kinds of content. Files also make up Mac OS X Lion; you typically do not interact with system files directly. Files have names that include filename extensions, such as .jpg and .doc (which can be hidden), and they are represented by icons in Finder windows and email attachments. Icons show a preview of what the file contains in their thumbnail images.

Like folders in the physical world, folders on a Mac are a means to organize things, such as files and other folders. Mac OS X Lion includes many folders by default. You can create, name, delete, and organize folders in any way you see fit (mostly any way—there are some folders you cannot or should not change). You open a folder in a Finder window to view its contents.

Working with Disks, Discs, Volumes, and Other Devices

Ultimately, your Mac manages data—lots and lots of data. It can use a number of types of devices to store and organize the data with which you work.

A disk drive, also known as a *hard drive*, is one type of physical device that Macs use to store data. A hard drive contains a magnetic disk accessed through a read/write head to read or store information. All Macs have at least one internal hard drive that contains the software it needs to work with Mac OS X Lion, applications you install, and documents you create. You can connect external disk drives to Macs through USB, FireWire, FireWire 800, or Thunderbolt ports to expand the available storage room. Drives come in various storage capacities, such as 750GB, 1TB, 2TB, and so on and operate at various speeds. Drives are represented on a Mac with icons that look different to represent different kinds of drives (internal versus external, for example).

Optical discs, namely CDs and DVDs, serve many purposes. Examples include listening to audio CDs, watching DVD movies and TV shows, and installing applications stored on a CD or DVD. You can also put your own data on CD or DVD, such as burning audio CDs with iTunes, creating DVDs with iDVD, and backing up your data on DVD. To use a disc, simply insert it into your Mac's DVD slot.

A *volume* is an area of a disk created using software rather than a physical space. A drive can be partitioned into multiple volumes, where each volume acts like a separate disk. A volume performs the same task as a disk, which is to store data. In fact, when you work with a volume, you might not be able to tell the difference. You can also access volumes being shared with you over a network. Some files (called *disk images*) appear as volumes that you use as if they were a volume on a disk. Volumes are used to organize data in different ways and to represent various resources you work with.

There are other kinds of devices on which you can store data, too, such as flash drives, digital cards, and so on. Mostly, these behave just like a hard drive, although they have much less storage capacity.

Using Menus

Menus contain commands that you can choose to perform various actions. All applications have their own menus, but most applications provide at least standard options, including File, Edit, View, and so on. Applications also have a menu that is named with the application's name. For example, the Finder menu appears when you are working on your desktop using the Finder application.

The Apple menu, located on the left end of the menu bar, is a special menu because it almost always appears regardless of what you are doing. It contains system-level commands that you might need at any time, which is why it is always available.

Using menus is straightforward. Point to the menu you want to use and click. The menu opens and you see the commands it contains. Some commands have sub-commands indicated by a right-facing triangle. When you point to such commands, additional commands appear. To make a selection on a menu, point to it so it becomes highlighted as shown in Figure 1.7 and click the mouse or trackpad button. The command to which you pointed is executed.

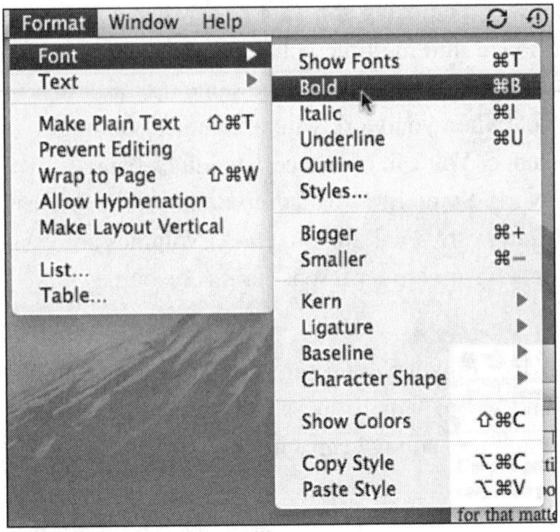

FIGURE 1.7   You work with menus extensively to perform different tasks in the applications you use.

Sleeping

When you aren't actively using your Mac, you can put it to sleep, which is a low-power mode. When a Mac sleeps, most of the processes stop, the display goes dark, and so on. To put a Mac to sleep, open the Apple menu and select Sleep, or if you use a mobile Mac, just close its lid. The Mac goes into sleep mode.

To wake it up, move the mouse, touch the trackpad, press a key, or open the lid (mobile Macs).

Logging Out

You can log out of your Mac when you are done using it. When you log out, all the open windows and applications on your desktop close and all processes stop. You end up at the Login window that you can use to log back in to the account you were using or in to a different account.

To log out, open the Apple menu and select Log Out *AccountName*, where *AccountName* is the name of the account you are using. Or you can press

Shift+cmd+Q. In the resulting dialog box, uncheck the **Reopen windows when logging back in** check box if you don't want the windows you are currently using to open again when you log back in (in other words, you pick up exactly where you left off). Click the **Log Out** button to complete the logout process.

Shutting Down

To turn your Mac off, you shut it down. When you shut down a Mac, all its processes stop. You only need to shut down your Mac when you won't be using it for a while; otherwise, log out or put it to sleep to enable you to get back to work much faster with one of those options because you won't have to power up your Mac again.

To shut down your Mac, open the Apple menu and select Shut Down. In the resulting dialog box, uncheck the **Reopen windows when logging back in** check box if you don't want the windows you are currently using to open again when you start the Mac again. Click the **Shut Down** button to complete the shutdown process.

Summary

In this lesson, you learned the fundamentals of using a Mac running Mac OS X Lion. In the next lesson, you learn how to work on the desktop using some of Lion's most useful features.

LESSON 2

Working on the Lion Desktop

In this lesson, you learn how to use the Lion desktop so you can work efficiently with your Mac.

Navigating the Desktop

The desktop is where all your Mac activities start; the Finder is the Mac application that provides the desktop and controls what you can do there. Figure 2.1 shows a typical desktop. The major elements with which you work are described in the following list:

▶ **Apple menu**. In the upper-left corner of the desktop is the Apple menu. As you learned in Lesson 1, "Getting Started with Mac OS X Lion," this menu is always on the far left end of the menu bar and contains system-level commands, such as those you use to shut down your Mac.

▶ **Menu bar**. At the top of the desktop is the menu bar. The first section of this (starting from the left side) is the menu bar for the application you are using. When you are working on the desktop, this is the Finder menu. When you are working with other applications, this menu is the name of the application. You learned how to use menus in Lesson 1.

▶ **Configurable menus**. Toward the middle and right side of the menu bar are configurable menus; these are configurable because you can determine whether they appear. For example, you can show or hide the Wi-Fi menu; when shown, you can use this menu to manage your Wi-Fi network connection.

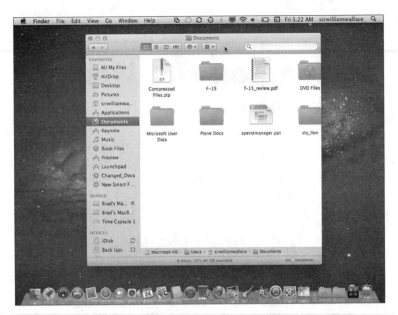

FIGURE 2.1   The desktop is the starting point for all your Mac activities.

▶ **Spotlight**. At the far right end of the menu bar is the Spotlight search tool, which has the magnifying glass icon. You learn about this later in this lesson.

▶ **Dock**. By default, the Dock is located on the bottom of the window (as you learn in Lesson 5, "Personalizing Lion," you can change its location). You learn about the Dock later in this lesson.

▶ **Finder window**. Finder windows show you the contents stored on your Mac; these include applications, folders, documents, and other files. You use Finder windows to move to, view, and take action on files and folders.

To perform a task, such as opening a document, you follow a similar pattern, which is the following:

1. Open a Finder window (if there isn't one open already).

2. Select the starting point.

3. Navigate to the end point.

4. Take action.

Sometimes, there are fewer steps. For example, if what you want to use is on the Dock, these steps collapse into one, which is to click the icon for what you want to open. And sometimes you start with a search instead of choosing a starting point, but the general flow of performing tasks is similar.

As you navigate, you move into and around in folders to get to the specific item with which you want to work. How you do this depends on the Finder window view you are using; you read more on these later in this lesson.

Working with Finder Windows

Because all the tasks you do start with the desktop and Finder application, it's important to understand how to work with Finder windows. Finder windows work a bit differently than other kinds of windows, such as those for applications and documents.

Using the Sidebar

Located on the left side of Finder windows, the Sidebar lets you easily get to specific locations. It comes with a number of default locations, but you can add items to or remove them from the Sidebar so that it contains the items you use most frequently.

The Sidebar is organized in sections as described in Table 2.1.

TABLE 2.1   Sidebar Sections

Section	Description
FAVORITES	This section contains locations on your Mac that you visit most frequently. FAVORITES includes a number of folders and other locations by default, but you can change the contents of this section to customize it. The contents of this section remain as you configure it.
SHARED	This section contains items you are accessing on a network, such as a shared hard disk or Time Capsule. The contents of this section change as you use different shared items.
DEVICES	This section contains hard disks, disk images, your iDisk, and so on that are mounted on your Mac. Like the SHARED section, the contents of this section change as the items with which you are working change.

To use an item on the Sidebar, click it. What happens when you click depends on the kind of icon you clicked. Examples of outcomes are provided in Table 2.2.

Each type of item of the Sidebar has a distinctive icon, making distinguishing what each icon represents easy.

You can show or hide the contents of each section. Point to the section's title and click Hide. The section is collapsed so you only see its title. Click Show to expand a section.

You can change the contents of the Sidebar using the following steps:

1. Select **Finder**, **Preferences**. The Finder Preferences window appears.

2. Click the **Sidebar** tab.

3. Check the check box for each item that you want to appear on the Sidebar.

4. Uncheck the check box for any items that you don't want to appear on the Sidebar.

5. Close the Finder Preferences window.

TABLE 2.2 Sidebar Icons

Icon	Action
All My Files	This icon causes all the files you've worked with to be shown in the Finder window. You can use the view and browse tools to access any file you want to work with.
AirDrop	When you click this icon, any Mac (running Mac OS X 10.7 or higher) that your Mac can communicate with using Wi-Fi appears with the icon of its current user. You can send files to other users by dropping them on the related icon; people can share files with you in the same way.
Devices	When you click a device, the contents of that device are displayed in the Finder window. For example, when you click a hard drive's icon, you see its contents.
Shared folder or drive	When you select a shared network resource, you either see the tools you can use to log in to that resource or you see the contents of the resource if your Mac is configured to log in to it automatically.
Folder	When you click a folder, you see its contents in the Finder window.
Document	Clicking a document's icon opens the associated application and you can see and work with the document's contents.
Application	If the icon is for an application, the application launches.
Search	If you click a search icon, the search runs and you see the results of the search in the Finder window.

You can also change the contents of the FAVORITES section by doing the following:

1. Open a Finder window.

2. To remove an item, perform a secondary click (one way is to hold the control key down while you click) on it and select **Remove from Sidebar**. The icon disappears. Of course, when you remove something from the Sidebar, it's not removed from the computer. The item remains in its current location on your Mac, but it is no longer accessible from the Sidebar.

3. To add something to the Sidebar, drag it from a Finder window or desktop onto the FAVORITES section. As you move the item onto the Sidebar, a blue line appears on the Sidebar at the location to which you've moved the item.

4. When you're over the location in which you want to place the item, release the button. The item's icon is added to the Sidebar, and you can use it just like the default items.

5. To change the order of items, drag them up or down the list. As you move an item, other items slide apart to show you where the item you are moving will be.

Using the Toolbar

The toolbar appears at the top of Finder windows and contains buttons and pop-up menus that you can use to access commands quickly and easily. It includes a number of default buttons and pop-up menus, but you can configure the toolbar so that it contains the tools you use most frequently. The default icons on the toolbar are described in Table 2.3 (from left to right).

TABLE 2.3   Toolbar Icons

Icon	Action
Back/Forward buttons	These buttons move you along the chain of Finder windows that you've moved through, just like Back and Forward buttons in a web browser.
View buttons	Use these to change the window view (more on this later in this lesson).
Action pop-up menu	This menu contains a number of useful contextual commands. These commands are the same as those that appear when you perform a secondary click on an item.
Arrange menu	This menu enables you to arrange the contents of the window. For example, you can group items by name, date last opened, size, and so on. Select None to remove the arrange settings.
Search bar	Use this to search for items with which you want to work.

> TIP: **Customizing the Toolbar**
>
> You can change the icons on the toolbar. Select **View, Customize Toolbar**. Remove icons by dragging them off the toolbar, or add items by dragging them onto the toolbar. Use the Show menu to change the toolbar's appearance. Click **Done** to save your changes.

Working with Finder Window Views

Finder windows offer different views of their contents. Each view works a bit differently and has advantages. To change views, open the view menu and select the view you want to use or click a view's icon on the toolbar (the view buttons are in the order as they are described from left to right on the toolbar). The views are as follows:

▶ **Icon**. In this view, contents appear as icons (refer to Figure 2.1) on which you double-click to open the related item (folder or file). The Icon view is the most pleasing to look at but offers the least information and functionality.

> TIP: **Customizing Views**
>
> Each view has options you can customize to suit your preferences. For example, you can change the size of icons shown in the Icon view. To customize a view, select **View, Show View Options**. Use the resulting dialog box to set the options for the view. If you click the **Use as Defaults** button, your customized view is used when you open new windows in that view.

► **List**. When in List view, contents of a window are shown in a list. You can sort items by clicking the column heading by which you want to sort the list; click it again to reverse the order. You can also expand or collapse the contents of folders by clicking the triangle that appears next to the folder's icon. Using the View Options, you can determine which columns of information appear. You can also drag columns to the left or right to change the order in which they appear. The List view is extremely useful because of the information it provides (see Figure 2.2).

FIGURE 2.2 The List view provides lots of information about the items you are viewing.

► **Columns**. The Columns view, as shown in Figure 2.3, is the best one for quickly navigating to any location on your Mac. In this view, contents appear in columns, so when you select a folder, its contents appear in a column to the right of the folder. Folder icons have a right-facing triangle on the right edge of the column. When you select a file, you see information about it, including a preview, if the file's contents can be shown in a preview. The path you are browsing is indicated by the shaded bar. You can change the width of columns by dragging their right edges to the left or right.

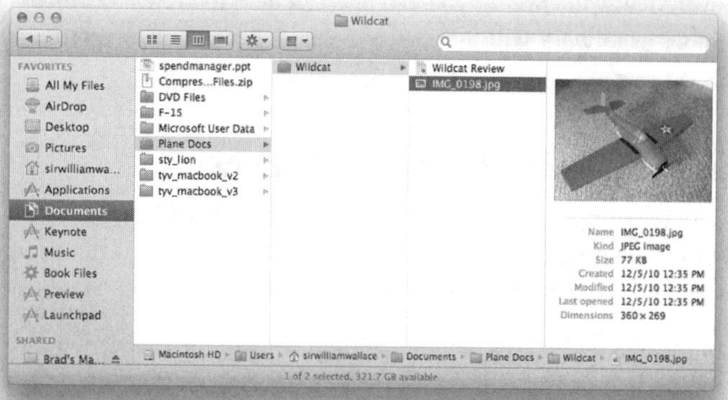

FIGURE 2.3   The Columns view provides the most efficient navigation.

▶ **Cover Flow**. The Cover Flow, as shown in Figure 2.4, sort of combines the Icon and List views. At the top of the window are thumbnails of the folders and files in the folder you are viewing. You can
flip through these by dragging across them, clicking on the left or
right side, or using the scrollbar that appears just below the thumbnails. The bottom section of the view is in List view, and this section works much like a window in that view. The thumbnail
directly facing you is in focus and is highlighted on the list.

FIGURE 2.4   The Cover Flow view shows a stack of files and folders you
can flip through.

Whichever view you choose, you can open an item to view its contents if it is a folder or to work with it in its associated application. Experiment with the various views to find the ones most useful to you.

Searching with Finder Windows

You'll end up with lots of files and folders on your Mac. Navigating directly to something of interest to you is not always easy. Fortunately, you can use Finder windows to search for items of interest to you. Here's how:

1. In the Search bar, located on the right edge of the Finder window toolbar, type what you want to search for. As you type, the Finder presents a menu of items that meet your search; these are organized by type of search, such as Filenames, Kinds, and so on. The results of the search are shown in the Finder window.

2. If the menu shows you what you want, you can jump directly to an item by clicking it on the list; if not, keep typing until you've entered all that you want to search for. As you type, the Finder continues to narrow the results shown in the window to match what you've typed.

3. You can change the location you are searching by clicking the buttons on the left side of the Search toolbar that appears when you perform a search. Options include This Mac, the folder currently selected, Shared, and so on.

4. To make what you are searching for more specific, click the **Add button** (+) located just under the Search bar. A new row appears in the Search toolbar.

5. Use the menus, text boxes, and date boxes to make your search more specific. For example, select Kind on the first menu and Document on the second menu to search for document files. The options that appear change based on what you select on the first menu.

6. Repeat steps 4 and 5 to add more search criteria. As you continue to refine your search, the content of the window is further reduced to show only those items that match your search.

TIP: **Saving Searches**

You can save a search by clicking the Save button just under the Search bar. Name the search and select the location in which you want to save it (the default is the Saved Searches folder). If you want the search to be placed on the Sidebar, check the **Add To Sidebar** check box. Click **Save** to save the search. You can perform the search again by clicking its icon on the Sidebar or moving to it in a Finder window and double-clicking on it.

NOTE: **Defaults**

The information on the Dock, Launchpad, Dashboard, and Mission Control in the following sections is based on default configurations. You can customize each of these elements to suit your preferences. For example, you can change the location of the Dock on the screen. Customizing these elements is explained in Lesson 5. Learn to use them as described in this lesson, and once you get comfortable, tailor them to work according to your own preferences.

Using the Dock

The Dock, as shown in Figure 2.5, provides one-click access to applications, folders, documents, and the Trash.

The Dock is an important part of your desktop. It is organized in two general sections. The area to the left of the application/document separation line (the white, dashed line that looks like a highway dividing line that is a few icons to the left of the Trash icon) contains application icons. On the right side of this line are icons for documents, folders, and minimized Finder or application windows and the Trash/Eject icon.

When folders appear on the Dock, by default they become stacks. When you click a stack, it pops up into a fan or appears as a grid (depending on how many items are in the folder) so that you can work with items it contains; an example is shown in Figure 2.6.

FIGURE 2.5   The Dock enables you to access applications, folders, and files with a single click.

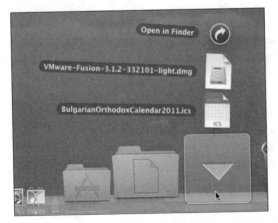

FIGURE 2.6   When you click a folder icon on the Dock, it expands on the desktop.

This has many purposes, including the following:

▶ Shows open applications (some applications are installed on the Dock and you always see their icons there). Application icons also provide information about what is happening with those applications. For example, when you receive email, the Mail application's icon changes to indicate the number of messages you have received since you last read messages.

▶ Enables you to open applications, folders, minimized windows, and documents quickly by clicking the related icon.

▶ Enables you to quickly switch among open applications and windows by clicking the icon for the item you want to bring to the front.

▶ Gets your attention. When an application needs your attention, its icon bounces on the Dock until you move into that application and handle whatever the issue is.

▶ Enables you to control an application and switch to any windows open in an application. When you perform a secondary click on the icon of an application, a pop-up menu appears. When the application is running, this menu lists commands as well as all the open windows related to that application. When the application isn't running, you see a different set of commands, such as the Open command you can use to open the application.

▶ Enables you to customize its appearance and function. You can store the icon for any item (applications, folders, and documents) on the Dock. You can control how the Dock looks, including its size; whether it is always visible; where it is located; and which applications, folder, and documents appear on it.

Two icons on the Dock are unique and are always on the Dock: the Finder and the Trash. When you click the Finder icon (anchored on the left end of a horizontal Dock or at the top of a vertical one), a Finder window opens if none is currently open. If at least one Finder window is open, clicking the Finder icon brings the Finder window you used most recently to the front.

The Trash icon stores the folders and files you delete. When the Trash contains files or folders, its icon includes crumpled paper so that you know the Trash is full. When you select an ejectable item, such as a DVD, the Trash icon changes to the Eject symbol. You can drag a disc or other ejectable item onto that icon to eject the disc, disk, or volume.

Unless an application is permanently installed on the Dock (in which case the icon remains in the same position), the icon for each application you open appears on the right (or bottom) edge of the application area of the Dock.

Unlike open applications, open documents don't automatically appear on the Dock. Document icons appear on the Dock only when you add them to the Dock manually or when you have minimized a document's window.

When you minimize a window, by default, the window becomes a thumbnail that moves onto the Dock. Minimized windows are marked with the related application's icon in the lower-right corner of the Dock icon so you can easily tell from which application the windows come.

When you quit an open application, its icon disappears from the Dock (unless you have added that application to the Dock so that it always appears there). Minimized windows disappear from the Dock when you maximize them or when you close the application from which a document window comes.

Using the Launchpad

The Launchpad provides one-click access to your applications. Click the Launchpad icon on the Dock (it is located just to the right of the Finder icon). The Launchpad fills the desktop and icons appear on the current page, as shown in Figure 2.7. To move to a different page, drag to the left or to the right or click on a page's dot at the bottom of the screen. As you drag, the page "flips" to the next page or to the previous page; if you click a dot, you jump to its page.

FIGURE 2.7 The Launchpad provides quick access to any application.

To open an application, click its icon. The Launchpad closes and you move into the application on which you clicked.

To access applications stored in a folder, click the folder. It expands so you can see the icons it contains. Click the icon you want to use.

TIP: **Launchpad Gestures**

If you use a trackpad, you can set a preference so you can open or close the Launchpad by pinching or unpinching on the trackpad with your thumb and three fingers. You can flip pages by dragging two fingers across the trackpad.

Using the Dashboard

The Dashboard contains widgets, which are small, single-purpose applications. The Dashboard is always running, so its widgets are always available to you. You can open the Dashboard in the following ways:

▶ Press Fn+F12 (default if you are using an Apple keyboard).

▶ Click the Dashboard's icon on the Dock (it looks like a gauge).

▶ Double-click the Dashboard's icon in the Applications folder.

▶ Open Mission Control and move all the way to the left.

When you open the Dashboard, the widgets that are configured to open when it is activated appear. You can then use those widgets or see their information.

When you finish using widgets, close the Dashboard again by pressing Fn+F12 (Apple keyboards) or by clicking the right-facing arrow in the lower-right corner of the window.

Using Mission Control

Mission Control is a tool that enables you to see and access anything on your desktop. When you open Mission Control, thumbnails are displayed at the top of the screen for the following items, as shown in Figure 2.8:

▶ Dashboard.

▶ Your desktops, named as Desktop X, where X is a sequential number; spaces are collections of applications and windows that you can create.

▶ Applications open in Full screen mode.

In the center part of the screen, all the windows open in the applications are shown on the current desktop. Windows are organized by application and the application's icon and name appear with its group.

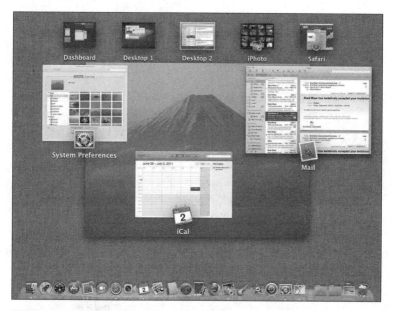

FIGURE 2.8 Mission Control shows you everything that's happening on your Mac.

TIP: **Mission Control Gestures**

If you use a trackpad, you can open Mission Control by dragging three or four fingers (depending on your preference, which you learn how to set in Lesson 5, "Personalizing Lion") up the trackpad; drag them down to close it. You can change spaces by dragging to the left or right.

To open Mission Control, open the Launchpad and then click the Mission Control icon, or, if you use a mobile Mac or Apple Wireless keyboard, press F3. To change what you are viewing, click its thumbnail. If you click a desktop, its windows appear in the center of the screen, and you can click on one to move into it. If you click the Dashboard, it opens. If you click an application in Full Screen mode, you move into it.

To move into a specific window, open the desktop in which it resides by clicking it and then click on the window into which you want to move.

Mission Control helps you manage screen clutter from open windows. It has three modes:

▶ **Hide all open windows**. This mode is useful when your desktop is so cluttered that you are having a hard time finding anything. Press the keyboard shortcut (the default is Fn+F11 if you are using an Apple keyboard). All the windows are moved off the screen, leaving an uncluttered desktop on which you can work. At the sides of the screen are the edges of the windows that have been moved off to the side. Press the keyboard shortcut or click anywhere in the shaded borders of the desktop to cause the windows to slide back onto the visible part of the desktop where you can use them again.

▶ **Open Mission Control to reduce all open windows to thumbnails**. This technique (which you learned about earlier) is useful when you have a lot of open windows and want to move into a specific one. You can reduce all your windows to thumbnails and then move into the window you want to use by clicking it. Press the keyboard shortcut (Fn+F9 by default), and all the windows in the current desktop appear. If you have more than one desktop defined (you learn how in Lesson 5), click the desktop on which the window you want to use appears and then click on the window you want to use.

▶ **Reduce an application's windows to thumbnails**. This mode is similar to the previous one, except that instead of showing all the open windows as thumbnails, it shows only the windows in the current application as thumbnails. Use this mode when you are working with multiple windows within the same application and want to jump to a specific one. Press the keyboard shortcut (Fn+F10 by default) to shrink all open windows for the current application so that they all fit on the desktop. The windows that are currently open appear as thumbnails toward the top of the screen. If you have closed windows (such as documents you are no longer using), they appear as smaller thumbnails toward the bottom of the screen. When you point to a window, it is high-lighted in blue to show it will become active when you click. To move into a window, click it. The window becomes active (if you click the window for a closed document, it opens) and moves to the front so that you can use it, and the rest of the open applica-tion windows move into the background.

Searching with Spotlight

Spotlight enables you to search your Mac a bit more completely than using the Search bar in Finder windows. The results are more organized, too. Do the following to use Spotlight:

1. Click the Magnifying glass icon in the upper-right corner of the window. The Spotlight tool opens.

2. Type what you want to search for. This can be literally anything, including text, dates, and so on. As you type, Spotlight shows the results of the search, organized in sections based on the types of results you've found. Results can include documents, emails, webpages, contacts, and so on.

3. Keep typing until you find the results for which you are looking.

4. Click a result to open it.

5. To move back to your results, press cmd+spacebar.

> TIP: **Web Search**
>
> You can move from searching your Mac to searching the Web by selecting one of the options shown in the Web Searches section.

Summary

In this lesson you learned how to manage the Lion desktop. In the next lesson, you learn how to install, use, and manage applications.

LESSON 3
Installing, Using, and Managing Applications

In this lesson, you learn how to install, use, and manage applications.

Using the App Store to Install and Update Applications

The App Store is an application whose purpose is to help you find, download, and install applications on your Mac. The great thing about the App Store is that it combines all these functions into one application so adding new applications to your Mac is a snap. It also helps you keep those applications current with the most recent release so you can be sure you are always using the latest and greatest version of your favorite applications.

The App Store enables you to browse for applications in a number of ways, and you can search for specific applications in which you are interested. You can view information about applications, such as screenshots, and when you want to get an application, you can do so with just a few clicks. The App Store application manages the process of downloading and installing the applications you buy so you don't have to do anything else to get the applications ready to use.

To download applications from the App Store, you need an Apple ID. If you've previously obtained an iTunes Store account or have ever made a purchase from the Apple Online Store, you already have an Apple ID and can use the same account to purchase applications. (If you don't have an Apple ID, you can use the App Store to get one of those, too.)

Configuring the App Store Application

To get started, open the App Store application and configure it to use your existing Apple ID or to create one for you. Here's how:

1. Click the **App Store** icon on the Dock. The App Store application opens (see Figure 3.1).

FIGURE 3.1   The App Store application makes finding, downloading, and installing applications a snap.

2. In the Quick Links section, click **Account**. The Sign In sheet appears.

> TIP: **Sign In Instead**
>
> If you already have an Apple ID and don't want to view your account information, click Sign In, enter your Apple ID and password, and click Sign In instead of using these steps.

3. If you already have an Apple ID, enter it and your password in their respective fields, and then click **View Account**; skip to

step 9. If you don't already have an Apple ID, continue to the next step.

4. Click **Create Apple ID**. You see the Welcome to the App Store screen, which is the first screen in an assistant that guides you through the creation of your Apple ID.

5. Click **Continue**.

6. Read and agree to the license conditions.

7. Provide the details for your Apple ID, such as email address, password, and so on; just follow the assistant's steps until you've provided all the required information. This includes a credit or debit card so you can pay for applications that have a license fee. When you finish, you have an Apple ID and password.

8. Go back to step 3.

9. Review your account information, and click **Done**. You are signed in to your account and are ready to shop in the App Store.

> TIP: **Changing Account Info**
>
> If you ever need to change your account information, view your account and click the Edit link for the information you want to change.

Finding, Downloading, and Installing Applications from the Mac App Store

The App Store provides three ways to browse for applications in which you are interested; the following tabs are available for your browsing pleasure:

▶ **Featured**. The Featured tab is sort of the home page for the App Store. It includes applications that are "new and noteworthy" and "hot," and there are several top 10 lists of apps there. You can also use the quick links area to get to categories of apps.

▶ **Top Charts**. As you probably suspect, this page contains applications grouped by various lists, such as Top Free, Top Paid, and so on.

▶ **Categories**. This one organizes applications by their categories, such as Productivity, Entertainment, Finance, and so on.

Using these tools is simple. Just click the tab at the top of the window that you want to use to browse. Then, click on links (graphics, text, and so on) to drill down within areas to get to individual applications of interest to you. After you're there, you can evaluate an application and download it (details are in the following paragraphs).

You can also search in the App Store for specific applications to download. Suppose you want to manage your finances on your Mac and have heard that iBank is a great personal finance tool (which it is by the way). To find, evaluate, and download iBank, perform the following steps:

1. Type **iBank** in the Search tool located in the upper-right corner of the App Store window and press Return. The application searches for applications associated with your search term and presents them on a list (in a specific search like this, you'll probably only find one or two, but if you perform a more general search, you'll get more results).

2. Click the application you want to evaluate. Its detail page opens, as shown in Figure 3.2.

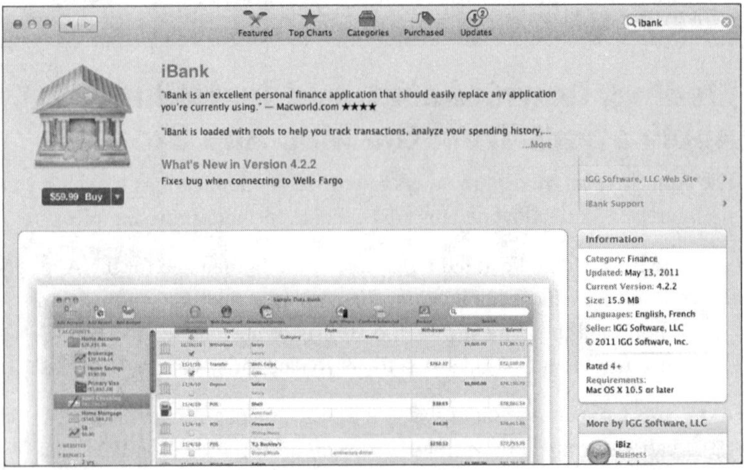

FIGURE 3.2   An application's detail page enables you to read about it, view screenshots, and so on.

3. Scroll around the screen and read the information, which includes a description of the application, screenshots of the application, customer ratings, and so on.

4. To download and install an application, click its **Buy** button if it has a license fee (the button shows the cost) or its **Free** button if it is a free application. (If it's a free application, you can skip the next two steps.)

5. If the application has a license fee, enter your Apple ID password and click **Sign In**.

6. Click **Buy**. (Check the check box if you don't want to see this prompt when you buy applications.)

The Launchpad opens and you see the application being downloaded to your Mac (see Figure 3.3). After download is complete, the application is installed for you and is ready to use.

FIGURE 3.3   On the Launchpad, you see the application being downloaded and installed.

NOTE: **Making Progress**
The progress of the download process is indicated on the application's icon and in the Launchpad icon on the Dock.

Updating Applications with the App Store Application

One of the best things about the App Store application is that it monitors the versions of the applications you have installed and lets you know when updates are available. When they are, you can use the App Store application to download and install them.

When updates are available, you see the number of updates available in a red circle on the App Store icon on the Dock. When you are ready to install the updates, open the App Store application and click the Updates tab (which also shows the number of available updates), as shown in Figure 3.4.

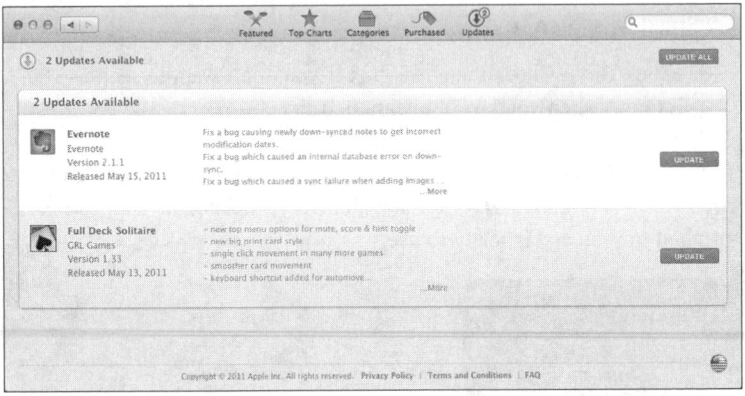

FIGURE 3.4   Use the Updates tab to download and install updates for the applications you've downloaded from the App Store.

To update all the applications, click **Update All**, or you can update individual applications by clicking each one's **Update** button. The download and installation process starts and a progress bar displays next to the application. When the process is complete, the Update button is replaced by the Installed graphic and the next time you run the application, you'll use the current version.

Installing Applications from the Mac App Store on Other Macs

The App Store application enables you to install applications you purchase on more than one Mac. Most applications don't include any protection features; the developers are relying on Mac users to be reasonable about their use of applications on multiple computers. In most cases, you can reasonably pay for one license for all the Macs you have in your home, for example, but if you use an application for business purposes, you really should purchase a copy for each Mac that is using it at the same time.

To install an application you've downloaded from the App Store on other Macs, perform the following steps:

1. Launch the App Store on the Mac on which you want to install the application.

2. Sign in to the App Store using the account under which the application was downloaded. If another account is already signed in, click **Account** and, in the resulting sheet, click **Sign Out**. Then sign in under the account associated with the application.

3. Click the **Purchased** tab. Here all the applications that have been downloaded under this account are shown. Applications that haven't been installed on the current computer have an Install button, while those that have been installed have the Installed graphic instead, as shown in Figure 3.5.

FIGURE 3.5 The Purchased tab lists all the applications that have been downloaded under the account signed in.

4. To install an application, click its **Install** button. The application is downloaded and the progress of the download is shown next to the application. When the process is complete, the application is ready to use.

Installing and Updating Applications from the Desktop

Unfortunately, not all Mac applications are available in the App Store. In those cases, you can obtain applications on a DVD or CD or download them from the Web. However you obtain them, there are two basic ways to install applications outside of the App Store app: using an installer application or via drag and drop.

Installing Applications with an Installer

Some applications include an installer application that you run to install the application. Using one of these is straightforward; simply launch the installer program and follow the onscreen instructions to complete the installation (see Figure 3.6 for an example).

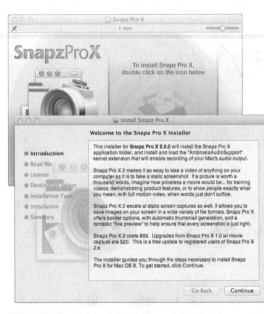

FIGURE 3.6   Using an installer application is mostly a matter of following onscreen instructions.

Installing Applications with Drag and Drop

Some applications are installed simply by dragging them onto the Applications folder and dropping them there. Many applications you download from the Web use this technique.

Download the application from the Web. The resulting file is typically a self-mounting disk image, which appears as a volume in the Devices section of the Sidebar. When the image has been downloaded and installed, a folder opens showing you what to do, as shown in Figure 3.7.

FIGURE 3.7   Firefox is an example of an application that you install by dropping its icon onto your Applications folder.

Open a new Finder window and either move into your Applications folder or select **Go**, **Applications**. Drag the application icon onto the Applications folder. It is installed; the progress of the process is shown on the screen. When it is done, the application is ready for use.

NOTE: **Disk Images**

If a disk image downloads but doesn't open automatically, double-click it.

Launching, Quitting, and Managing Applications

If you have used the Mac App Store application, you already have the basics of using applications down. In this section, you get more information to help you use applications even more effectively.

Launching Applications

The first step to using an application is to start it, more commonly called *launching* or *opening* it. There are many ways to do this, including the following:

▶ Click its icon on the Dock.

▶ Click its icon on the Sidebar.

▶ Open the Launchpad and click its icon.

▶ Open the Applications folder and double-click its icon.

▶ Open a document with which the application is associated.

▶ Configure it to be opened automatically when you log in to your user account.

▶ Click a link tied to the application, such as a URL to open a Web browser or a link to a song to open iTunes.

You'll probably use several of these methods as you work with your Mac. Generally, you want the applications you use most to be available on the Dock because it is almost always available to you. If you always or almost always have an application open (such as an email application), configure your user account so that it opens whenever you log in to your account; that way, you seldom have to launch it manually. (See Lesson 9, "Configuring and Managing User Accounts," to learn how to do this.)

Managing Open Applications

You'll likely be running multiple applications at the same time, and Mac OS X is designed to do this. However, having lots of applications open means many windows will be open on your desktop; managing all these applications and windows can be a challenge.

An important concept to understand about running multiple applications is that one application is frontmost or active at any one time. The other applications continue to run in the background, but you aren't actively using them. The open applications and the windows open in those applications are "stacked" on top of each other, and you can usually see multiple windows at the same time. The active application and window are the ones "on top" of the stack (frontmost).

There are a couple of ways to tell which application is active. First, notice the menu bar at the top of the screen. It always shows the active application's menu; the first choice to the right of the Apple menu is the name of the active application. Second, look for the window with the three buttons (close, minimize, and zoom) in color; this indicates the active window. Windows in the background have these buttons, but the buttons contain no color. For example, in Figure 3.8, the window titled All My Files is active and the window called Documents is open but is in the background. Notice that the item next to the Apple menu is Finder, showing that the Finder is the active application.

FIGURE 3.8   Understanding how windows and applications are stacked in the desktop helps you manage your applications more effectively.

You can move into any window by clicking in it. When you do, it moves to the front and the application providing it becomes active so you can use it.

Also realize that an application can be active (at the top of the stack) but have no open windows. In this case, you only see the application's menu at the top of the screen, even though it doesn't have any windows associated with it. If other windows are open, you might see them "underneath" the active application.

Almost all applications allow you to have multiple windows open at the same time, too. For example, you might be working on multiple documents simultaneously or need to copy and paste parts of one document into another. Like applications on the desktop, open windows within an application are stacked on top of each other, with the window on top being the active one. An application's Window menu enables you to see the names of its open windows; choose a window on this menu to bring it to the front.

With multiple applications running and many windows open, it can be difficult to know exactly which is "on top," and you might not be able to see the window you want to move into in order to click in it to bring it to the front. Fortunately, Mac OS X Lion includes a number of features to help you manage multiple applications and lots of windows, including the following:

▶ **Mission Control**. Mission Control enables you to quickly move into any open application and into any window within those open applications. Mission Control is explained in Lesson 2, "Working on the Lion Desktop."

▶ **Desktops**. Desktops are collections of applications that you create based on how you use applications. You can switch between applications easily by changing desktops through Mission Control. Doing so is also explained in Lesson 2.

▶ **Window management**. Mission Control also helps you manage the windows on your desktop by moving all the windows off to the side so you can see a clean desktop or showing you all the open windows within an application so you can easily move into one of them. As you might guess, this feature of Mission Control is covered in Lesson 2 as well.

▶ **Application Switcher**. The Application Switcher enables you to jump into any open application using the keyboard. To use the Application Switcher, press cmd+Tab. The Application Switcher appears as shown in Figure 3.9. Icons for each running application are shown; the application that you will move to when you move out of the Switcher is highlighted in a white box and its name is shown under the icon. To move to a different application, press Tab or Shift+Tab while holding down the cmd key. When the application you want to move into is highlighted with the box, release the keys. That application becomes the active application, and you move into the window you worked in most recently. (You can also click an application's icon to move into it.)

FIGURE 3.9   Use the Application Switcher to quickly jump into any open application.

Another useful tool to manage applications is the contextual menu that appears when you perform a secondary click (one way to do this is to hold down the control key and click) on an application's icon on the Dock. If the application is running, a menu displays that enables you to move into any window with the application or to access its commands. For example, Figure 3.10 shows the contextual menu for Mail.

TIP: **Open Applications**

The icons for open applications always appear on the Dock. If they are installed on the Dock, they appear where they are installed. If not, they appear to the left of the dashed dividing line. In either case, you can jump back into an application and make it active by clicking its icon on the Dock.

FIGURE 3.10 Open an application's contextual menu on the Dock to control it or jump into any of its windows.

Quitting Applications

When you're done with an application, you can quit it. The benefit of quitting an application is that it no longer uses any resources (processor or active memory) and it removes some of the clutter from the desktop because when you quit an application, all its windows close. The downside of quitting an application is the time it takes to restart the application, so you should only quit an application when you won't be using it again for a while. (You'll probably leave some applications, such as email, running all the time.)

> TIP: **Hiding Applications**
>
> If you want to keep an application open but move it out of the way, use the Hide *application* command on the *application* menu, where *application* is the name of the application. When you hide an application, it (and all the windows open in it) disappears from the desktop but continues to run in the background. You can move back into the application using the Application Switcher or by clicking its icon on the Dock. The shortcut for the Hide command is cmd+H. If you press Option+cmd+H, all applications except for the active one are hidden.

There are two ways to quit an application. When an application is working normally, use the Quit command on the *application* menu, where *application* is the name of the application, or press cmd+Q. The application stops running; if you have open documents with unsaved changes, you are prompted to save the changes before the application quits. When the application stops, all its windows close and its icon disappears from the Dock unless it is installed there.

When an application isn't working correctly and is hung (meaning it appears to be active but does not respond to any commands), you can force it to quit. (A hung application is usually accompanied by a spinning, colored wheel.) You should only do this after waiting a few minutes to make sure the application is actually hung and that there just isn't some process slowing things down. When you are sure the application is hung, you can force it to quit.

> CAUTION: **Force Quits**
> When you force an application to quit, you lose unsaved changes in all its open documents. So, don't force quit unless you are sure the application is completely hung.

There are a couple of common ways to force an application to quit:

- ▶ Open the application's contextual menu on the Dock and select Force Quit (this command appears only when the application is hung, which is indicated by the text "Not Responding").

- ▶ Open the Apple menu and select Force Quit or press Option+cmd+Power key. In the resulting dialog box, select the application that is not responding (it will be highlighted in red) and click Force Quit. Click Force Quit at the prompt.

When you force an application to quit, move into the other open applications and save your documents. Then, restart your Mac.

Working with Documents

Many applications exist to create documents, such as text documents in a word processor, spreadsheets, graphics, and so on. In this section, you learn some of the ways to work with documents.

Opening Documents

There are a number of ways to open a document, including the following:

▶ Double-click its icon on the desktop.

▶ Open the application associated with the document; select File, Open; move to and select the document; and click Open.

▶ Open the File menu and select Open Recent; on the resulting menu, select the document. (This only works if you've opened the document recently, which is defined differently in various applications.)

▶ Open the Apple menu, select Recent Items, and select the document you want to open. (A document appears as long as you've opened in within the set number of items, which is 10 by default.)

TIP: **Recent Items**
You can set the number of recent items on the Apple menu using the General pane of the System Preferences application. Select the number of recent documents you want to show on the Documents menu.

When you open a document, the application with which the document is associated opens and you can start working with it.

TIP: **New Documents**
To create a new document, open the application in which you want to create it, and select File, New. A new, empty document window appears. Save the document using the information in the following section.

Saving Documents

As you work with documents, you'll probably want to save your work. Use the Save command on the File menu to do this. How this works depends on whether an application has been updated to support Lion's document version feature, which is explained in the next section, and if you've saved the document previously.

The first time you save a document, you actually use the Save As command. When you use applications that haven't been fully updated for Lion, Save As appears as a separate command on the File menu while updated applications have only the Save command on their File menus. If you haven't saved the document before, select the Save or Save As command on the file menu. The Save As sheet appears as shown in Figure 3.11.

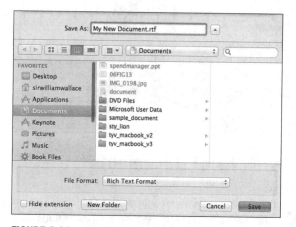

FIGURE 3.11   The first time you save a document, name it and choose the location in which you will save it.

TIP: **Save Locations**

The Save As sheet has two modes. One enables you to navigate anywhere on your Mac; this is the mode shown in Figure 3.11. In the other mode, you see the Where menu instead of the center navigation area. The Where menu presents specific locations you can choose as the save location for the new file. To switch between the modes, click the triangle just to the right of the Save As box.

Give the document a name in the Save As box. Choose the location in which you will save it using the center part of the sheet; this works just like navigating in Finder windows. Then, select options for the document, such as its format. When you are ready to save the document, click Save.

The document's window is renamed with the filename you entered and is ready for you to work with.

As you work with your document, you should regularly save it by selecting File, Save a Version; selecting File, Save; or pressing cmd+S. Whether the command you use is Save a Version or Save depends on if the application supports Lion's versioning feature. It if does, the command is Save a Version, which is explained in the next section. If it doesn't, the command is Save, in which cases the version you save replaces the previous version.

> TIP: **Saving Documents**
>
> If a document supports Lion's version feature, a version is saved automatically every hour or when you make significant changes. If an application does not support this feature, you should save it regularly. Some applications provide an automatic save feature; if an application you use has this feature, you should configure it to save your document frequently.

Managing Versions of Documents

Mac OS X Lion includes a versioning feature that helps you manage versions of your documents. When applications support this feature, a version of your documents is automatically saved every hour or when you make significant changes. This helps you avoid losing any work you have done, plus you can go back to any previous version to use it instead.

> NOTE: **Version Support**
>
> To tell whether a document you use supports Lion's Versioning feature, open its File menu when you have a document open. If the Save a Version command displays, the application does support Lion Versioning. If the command shown is Save, the application doesn't support Versioning.

To return a document to an earlier version, perform the following steps:

1. With the document open, select File, Revert to Saved. The application's interface is replaced by the version tool, as shown in Figure 3.12. On the left is the current version of the document.

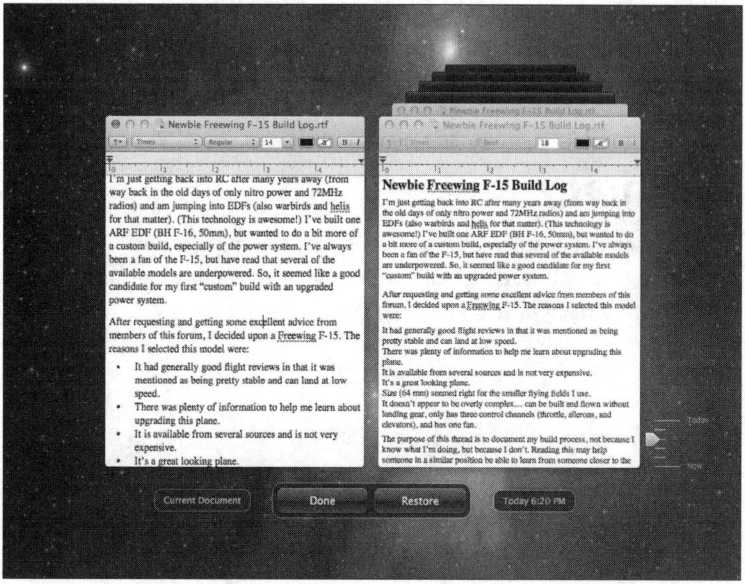

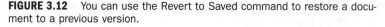

FIGURE 3.12 You can use the Revert to Saved command to restore a document to a previous version.

On the right is the other versions that have been saved, starting with the most recent on top and moving back in time toward the back of the screen. In the lower-right corner of the screen, the version timeline shows you how far back in time the document goes. The date and time of the version being displayed on the right is indicated under its thumbnail.

2. To go back to a previous version of a document, click its title bar or click on an earlier version on the timeline. The version you selected comes to the front.

3. Scroll in the older version to compare it to the current version (which you can scroll in, too).

4. To restore an earlier version, with the version to which you want to restore the document on the front of the stack on the right side of the screen, click **Restore**. The version of the document you selected replaces the version that existed when you selected the Revert to Saved command.

5. To keep the current version, click **Done** instead. You return to the document as it was when you selected the Revert to Saved command.

Summary

In this lesson you learned how to install, use, and manage applications. In the next lesson, you learn about some of the great applications that are included with Mac OS X Lion.

LESSON 4

Touring Lion's Applications

In this lesson, you take a tour of some of the most useful applications that are included with Mac OS X Lion.

Understanding Mac OS Lion's Applications

Mac OS X Lion is an operating system, which means it provides the software that runs Macintosh computers. However, Lion also includes quite a number of applications that you can use for many things. The following sections provide an overview of some of the applications you might find useful or fun.

Most of Mac OS X's applications are stored in the Applications folder, which you can access on the Sidebar by pressing Shift+cmd+A or choosing **Go**, **Applications**. Some applications are stored within the Utilities folder that is stored within the Applications folder; you can jump into it by choosing **Go**, **Utilities** or pressing Shift+cmd+U.

NOTE: **Other Application Locations**

Applications can also be stored within the Applications folder in a user's Home folder. These applications are available only to the user in whose folder they are stored or to users who have permissions to access that folder. Some system applications are stored in various locations within the startup volume, such as in the System folder, but you don't interact with those applications directly.

Like other Mac applications, you can open Lion's applications in many ways, including the following:

▶ Click their icons on the Dock.

▶ Open the Launchpad and click an application's icon (if the application is in the Utilities folder, click that icon to open the folder and then click the application's icon).

▶ Open the Applications (or Utilities) folder and double-click the application's icon.

▶ Open a document with which an application is associated.

NOTE: **Where Are They?**

All the applications described in the following sections are located in the Applications folder unless otherwise noted.

Previewing Documents with Preview

As you might be able to guess from its name, Preview enables you to view (or preview if you will) documents. Preview is quite versatile as far as the type of files you can view with it. It is Lion's default viewer application for Portable Document Format (PDF) files (as shown in Figure 4.1) and many types of images. Some of its useful features include the following:

▶ **PDF editing and annotation tools**. Preview enables you to view PDF documents, but you can also annotate them with notes, highlights, and so on. This is useful for reviewing PDF documents because you can add information to the PDF without affecting the original document.

▶ **Image rotation**. You can rotate images in any direction.

▶ **Image cropping**. When you are viewing an image, you can drag over part of it and choose **Tools**, **Crop** to crop the image so it includes only the part you selected.

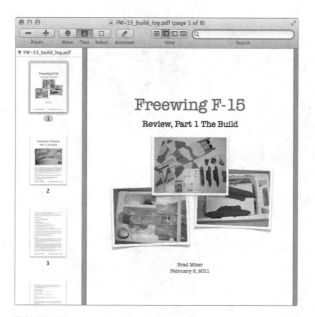

FIGURE 4.1   Preview is a useful application for viewing PDFs, images, and other kinds of documents.

> ▶ **Slideshow**. When you open multiple images or documents, you can view them in a slideshow by choosing **View**, **Slideshow**.

NOTE: **Saving in Preview**

You can save documents within Preview using its Save command on the File menu. For example, if you annotate a PDF, you might want to save a version with your notes separately from the original.

Storing Contact Info with the Address Book

The Address Book is just what it sounds like, which is a tool to help you store and organize your contact information (see Figure 4.2). But that's

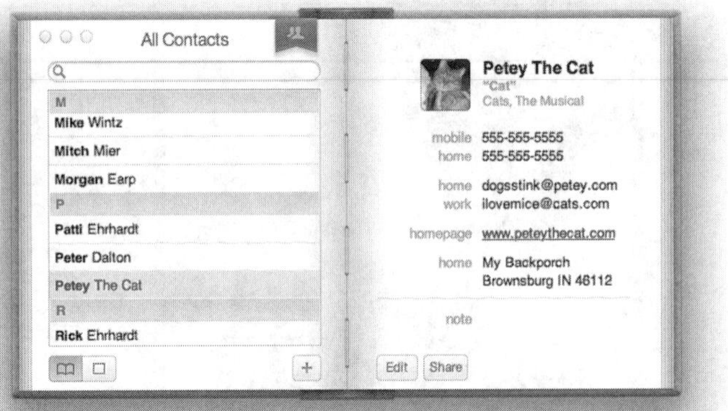

FIGURE 4.2   Address Book is great for keeping your contacts current and easily available.

just a start for Lion's Address Book. Some of its key features include the following:

▶ **Synchronize**. With iCloud or MobileMe, you can synchronize your Address book with other Macs, iPhones, iPod touches, iPads, and Windows PCs so you have access to your contacts no matter which device you happen to be using.

▶ **Use vCards**. Address Book uses the vCard standard. You can add contact information by dragging a vCard onto the Address Book window; you can also drag a contact onto the desktop to create a vCard from it.

▶ **Print Envelopes and Labels**. Address Book enables you to print on envelopes and many types of labels.

▶ **Share**. When you view a contact, you can easily share its information by clicking the Share button. An email is created with the contact's information attached.

▶ **Subscribe**. Address Book users can subscribe to each others' Address Books to share contact information.

► **Store lots of information**. You can add many kinds of information to each contact stored in Address Book, including multiples of the same information, such as email addresses.

> NOTE: **Google and Yahoo!**
> You can synchronize your Address Book contacts with Google and Yahoo!, too.

Enjoying DVD Content with DVD Player

The DVD Player application enables you to watch DVDs on your desktop. It includes most of the features you expect in a modern DVD player.

> NOTE: **No Blu-ray**
> Unfortunately, at this time, standard Mac DVD drives don't support Blu-ray discs.

Communicating with FaceTime

FaceTime is an application created initially for the iPhone, but it's now supported on Macs. With it, you can have face-to-face conversations with other Mac, iPhone, iPod touch, or iPad users. All you need is an Apple ID and a Mac equipped with a FaceTime-compatible camera (all current MacBook and iMac models include one).

When you launch the FaceTime window and log in to your account, you see two panes. In the left pane is a preview of the image you are broadcasting. In the right pane, you see your contact information from Address Book.

To place a FaceTime call, you simply click the email address or phone number of the person with whom you want to chat. If the person accepts the call, her image fills the FaceTime window while your preview shrinks to a thumbnail (which you can move around the screen).

That's all there is to it. FaceTime works really well and is a great way to communicate with people you can't see in person.

Managing Your Time with iCal

iCal is Lion's time-management application, as shown in Figure 4.3.

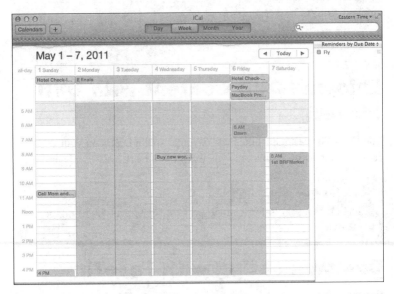

FIGURE 4.3   iCal enables you to manage your time and to access published calendars.

Of course, iCal enables you to create events and to-do items. However, it does much more, such as the following:

▶ **Tracking multiple calendars**. You can create multiple calendars and manage them all in one place.

▶ **Publishing and subscribing to calendars**. One of iCal's most useful features is the ability to publish your calendars so other iCal users can subscribe to them. Of course, you can subscribe to other iCal users' calendars, too. Calendars to which you are sub-scribed appear in the window along with your calendars. You can use colors to make the calendars easier to distinguish. The great thing about publishing a calendar is that it is read-only; others can view your calendars, but they can't change them.

▶ **Sharing calendars**. This feature enables you to share your calendars with others. Sharing a calendar is similar to subscribing to one except that people with whom you share a calendar can make changes to it.

▶ **Synchronizing calendars**. Like Address Book, you can use iCal to synchronize your calendars on multiple devices.

▶ **Managing group events**. iCal supports invitations and calendar status so you can invite other people to your events while seeing their availability. iCal also tracks who accepts or rejects your invitations.

NOTE: **Public Calendars**

Some organizations, such as sports teams, publish a calendar to which you can subscribe. Check out http://www.apple.com/downloads/macosx/calendars/ to see if there any calendars of interest to you.

Playing Digital Music and Video with iTunes

iTunes is one of the most widely used applications among Mac users, and many Windows users too, for good reason. iTunes enables you to store, organize, and enjoy all sorts of digital content, including music, audiobooks, podcasts, movies, TV shows, and so on (see Figure 4.4). You can access the iTunes Store to buy or rent all sorts of great content, which is downloaded to your iTunes Library. Plus, iTunes is a required companion for iPods, iPod touches, and iPads.

Here's a quick list of just some of iTunes' great features:

▶ iPod, iPod touch, and iPad management

▶ Smart and standard playlists

▶ Podcast subscriptions

▶ Genius playlists

▶ The iTunes Store

FIGURE 4.4 iTunes is a great application with which you can listen to music, watch video, and much more.

- ▶ Content streaming
- ▶ Home sharing
- ▶ Audiobooks
- ▶ Internet radio
- ▶ Ping

> NOTE: **It Would Take a Book...**
>
> iTunes is a great application and it would take a book to tell you all about it. If you're interested in learning more, see my book *Sams Teach Yourself iTunes 10 in 10 Minutes*.

Managing Email with Mail

Email is an essential part of most people's lives these days. Fortunately, Lion includes Mail, which is a full-featured email application and is shown in Figure 4.5.

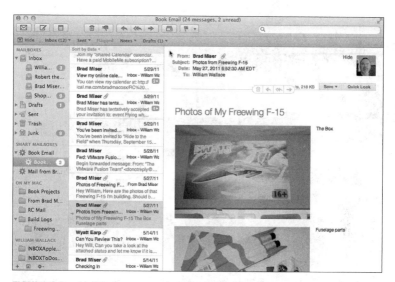

FIGURE 4.5   Mail helps you make the most of email.

Mail offers many great email tools. It supports many types of email accounts and of course enables you to compose, read, and organize email. It also offers email rules to automatically manage your email along with a host of other features you might find handy.

Surfing the Web with Safari

It would be hard to argue that the Web is one of the most significant technologies ever created. Lion's Safari Web browser equips you to take advantage of all the Web has to offer (see Figure 4.6). In addition to being a full-featured Web browser, Safari offers great performance and stability, along with some outstanding features, such as

▶ **Top Sites**. Safari automatically builds a collection of the sites you visit regularly so you can return to a site just by clicking its thumbnail. You can also add sites to this page manually.

▶ **Bookmarks**. You can quickly create and organize bookmarks to provide fast access to your favorite sites.

▶ **Tabs**. Safari supports tabs so you can have multiple sites open in one browser window.

FIGURE 4.6   Safari's Top Sites page makes returning to your favorite websites fast and easy.

Being Creative with the iLife Suite

Technically speaking, iLife isn't a default Lion application because it doesn't come as part of the operating system; it is installed on most Macs by default, or you can purchase it from Apple. And iLife isn't even an application; it's a suite of applications, including:

▶ **iPhoto**. This is a great application for storing, editing, and organizing digital photos. But, that's just the start. You can also share photos on the Web, create projects (such as photo books and slideshows), get your photos professionally printed, and much more. See Figure 4.7 for a quick look at iPhoto.

▶ **iMovie**. This is a digital video editing application. You can add video clips to a project and then make a movie from those clips by adding transitions, titles, special effects, and audio tracks. After you've created your masterpiece, you can watch and share it in many ways.

▶ **GarageBand**. This application enables you to play and record music. You can use the many digital instruments it includes, and

FIGURE 4.7   iPhoto stores, organizes, edits, and shares your photos.

you can connect your Mac to real instruments to record them. Your music can include multiple tracks mixed to perfection.

▶ **iWeb**. This application helps you create your own web pages, quickly and easily. If you are a MobileMe user, you can publish your sites with a single click.

▶ **iDVD**. Use iDVD to put your content on professional-looking DVDs, including custom menus with sound and visual effects.

Summary

In this lesson you toured some of the great applications that come with Mac OS X Lion. In the next lesson, you learn how to personalize Lion.

LESSON 5

Personalizing Lion

In this lesson, you learn how to make your Mac your own by personalizing Mac OS X Lion.

Setting Finder Preferences

Just like other applications, the Finder has a set of preferences that you can configure to change the way it works and looks. To access Finder Preferences, open the Finder menu and select Preferences or press cmd+,. The Finder Preferences dialog box has four tabs; the options provided on these tabs are shown in Table 5.1.

TABLE 5.1   Finder Preferences

Tab	Elements	Description
General (see Figure 5.1)	Show check boxes	Use these check boxes to determine whether icons for the associated items are shown on your desktop. For example, if you check the Hard Disks check box, icons for each hard disk your Mac can access are shown on the desktop; you can open a disk by double-clicking its icon.
	New Finder windows show	Use the pop-up menu to determine the initial location shown in new Finder windows. For example, if you select All My Files, whenever you open a new Finder window, you see a window containing all your files. You can select other locations, such as the Desktop or Document folders, or select Other and select any folder.
	Always open folders in a new window	Check this check box to cause a new window to open every time you open a folder, such as by clicking its icon.

TABLE 5.1 Finder Preferences

Tab	Elements	Description
	Spring-loaded folders and windows	When this check box is checked and you hover over a folder, it springs open so you can work with it, such as to place a file in it. Use the slider to set the amount of delay time between when you hover over a folder and when it springs open.
Labels	Label colors and text fields	On this tab, you can define labels that include a color and text. You can apply your labels to files and folders to help keep them organized and to help you identify them. Change the text for each color to be the labels you want to use. To apply labels, select files or folders, perform a secondary click, and select the label you want to apply.
Sidebar	Check boxes	Check the check boxes to show the associated items on the Sidebar; uncheck an item's check box to remove it from the Sidebar (the item itself is not affected). For example, to show your iDisk on the Sidebar, check the iDisk check box.
Advanced	Show all filename extensions	Check this check box to show the extensions appended to filenames (the period and the code that indicates the type of file it is). If this is unchecked, the filename extensions are hidden. You can override this setting on individual files and folders.
	Show warning before changing an extension	With this check box checked, when you change a filename extension, you see a warning prompt. This can be useful so you don't unintentionally change an extension, which can render a file useless.
	Show warning before emptying the Trash	This check box causes a warning prompt to appear when you empty the Trash.

TABLE 5.1   Finder Preferences

Tab	Elements	Description
	Empty Trash Securely	With this check box checked, when you empty the trash, the files you are deleting are overwritten, making them harder to recover. The downside of this is that it takes longer to empty the trash, but it is a more secure way to get rid of files.
	When performing a search	Use this pop-up menu to select the default search location. For example, to search your entire Mac, select Search This Mac, or to search the current folder, select Search the Current Folder. You can override it during searches.

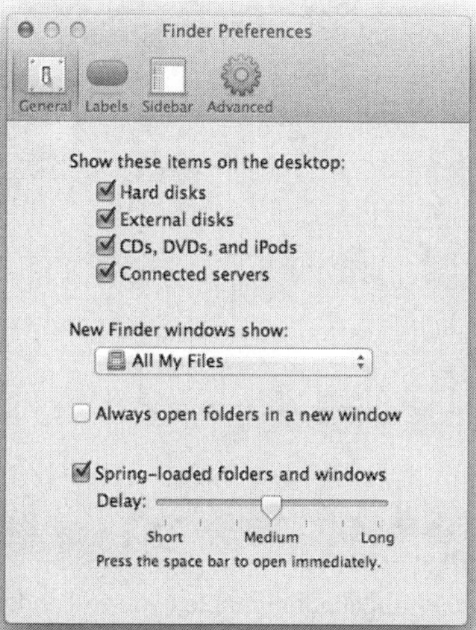

FIGURE 5.1   Use the General tab of the Finder Preferences dialog box to set icon view and folder action preferences.

Working with the System Preferences Application

The System Preferences application enables you to configure many aspects of Mac OS X Lion. The application is organized into panes, based on the specific areas you can configure, as shown in Figure 5.2. To configure an area's preferences, click the icon for that area and use the resulting controls to configure that area. For example, to set the sound preferences for your Mac, click the **Sound** icon and use the tools on the resulting Sound pane to configure sound-related aspects of Mac OS X Lion.

FIGURE 5.2 The System Preferences application enables you to configure many aspects of how Mac OS X Lion works and looks.

NOTE: **Other Preferences**

The default Mac OS X Lion preferences are organized in categories by default, such as Personal, Hardware, and so on. Some software and hardware also has preferences you set through the System Preferences application. These panes appear in the Other category (in Figure 5.2, you shows see the preference icon for Adobe's Flash Player software in the Other category).

The following sections provide information on some of the more commonly used preference panes. You'll find detailed information about others in the related lessons; for example, the Print & Scan pane is explained in Lesson 7, "Installing and Using Printers." When you have learned to use the panes explained in this and the other lessons, you'll also be able to use the other panes because the general steps are similar.

NOTE: **Authentication**

Some panes require that you be authenticated under an administrator account before you can make changes. If the pane has the lock icon in the lower-left corner, you must be authenticated to use it. If the lock is closed, click it, enter an administrator username (if necessary), enter the password for the administrator user account, and click Unlock. The lock icon "opens," indicating you are authenticated and are able to change the pane's settings.

Setting a Desktop Picture

The desktop picture is what you see "behind" folders and windows that are open on the desktop. Mac OS X Lion includes a number of images you can use as your desktop picture, but it's even more fun when you use your own images. To configure desktop pictures, perform the following steps:

1. Open the Desktop & Screen Saver pane.

2. Click the **Desktop** tab, as shown in Figure 5.3 (the selected image is shown as the desktop picture in the background).

3. Select the source of images containing the image you want to apply to your desktop. For example, to use one of Mac OS X's default images, select **Desktop Pictures**; to use your own photos, click **iPhoto**. Thumbnails of the images in the source you selected appear in the right part of the window.

FIGURE 5.3 Setting a desktop picture makes your Mac more interesting to look at.

TIP: **Expand or Collapse**

To expand or collapse any of the sources shown, click the triangle next to the item's name. When this triangle points to the right, the item is collapsed and its contents are hidden. When the triangle points down, the item is expanded and you see its contents.

4. Click the image you want to use as your desktop picture. It is applied to the desktop. A thumbnail of the currently applied picture is shown in the Image well at the top of the pane.

5. To have the picture change automatically, check the **Change picture** check box and on the pop-up menu, select how often you want the image to change.

6. If you performed step 5, check **Random Order** if you want the images to appear in random order instead of the order they are in the selected source.

7. To make the menu bar somewhat transparent so you see the desktop picture behind it, check the **Translucent menu bar** check box.

TIP: **Multiple Displays**

If you use multiple displays with your Mac, you can set a different desktop picture on each.

Configuring the Dock

In Lesson 2, "Working on the Lion Desktop," you learned how to use the Dock. The Dock pane, as shown in Figure 5.4, enables you to configure where the Dock is located and some aspects of how it works. The options are explained in Table 5.2.

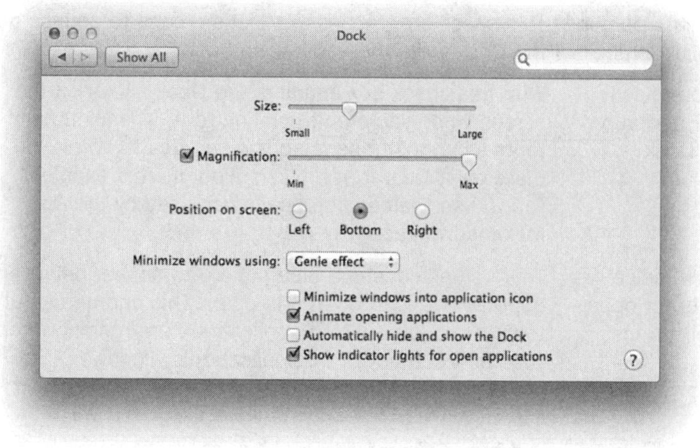

FIGURE 5.4   You can configure the Dock to make it even more useful.

TABLE 5.2 Dock Preferences

Control	What It Does
Size slider	Sets the default Dock size, which is the size it is when only applications whose icons are installed there are open and no windows are minimized. The Dock's size changes automatically as you open applications and minimize windows; the slider controls the Dock's "starting" size.
Magnification	This check box and slider cause icons on the Dock to enlarge when you point to them, making them easier to identify. Check the check box and use the slider to set the amount of magnification.
Position on screen	These radio buttons determine where the Dock is located.
Minimize windows using	The settings on this menu determine how windows move onto the Dock when you minimize them. The options are Genie effect and Scale effect.
Minimize windows into application icon	With this check box checked, when you minimize windows, their icons move onto the Dock icon of the application providing the window instead of onto a separate icon on the Dock.
Animate opening applications	This check box causes application icons to bounce on the Dock while the application opens.
Automatically hide and show the Dock	With this check box enabled, the Dock slides off the screen when you aren't pointing to it; when you point to its location, it opens so you can use it. When you move away from it again, it is hidden. This enables you to use the desktop space occupied by the Dock for window space.
Show indicator lights for open applications	This setting causes a blue sphere to appear below an application's icon when it is open. This can be useful to help you know which applications are running when you can't see any of an application's windows.

Configuring the Display

Your Mac's display is capable of showing you visual information at different resolutions; a resolution is a number of pixels (short for *picture elements*) horizontally by a number of pixels vertically. For example, a resolution of 1024X768 is commonly used as the smallest resolution that most applications support. The larger the resolution, the more working space you have on the screen, but the smaller each pixel appears, which means the overall image appears smaller.

The specific resolutions your Mac supports depend on the type of hardware it has and the display it uses. To determine which resolution is best for you, follow these steps:

1. Open some windows on your desktop, such as a text document and webpage.

2. Open the Displays pane of the System Preferences application.

3. Click the **Display** tab. The Resolutions box shows all the resolutions that your Mac and its display support, starting with the highest resolution at the top of the list.

4. Click the resolution you want to try, such as **1152X720**. The desktop and the open windows are resized to the resolution you selected.

CAUTION: **Resolution Warning**

If you select a resolution and see a warning prompt, it's a good idea to heed that warning and select a different resolution. Choosing a resolution that Lion warns you is not a good choice can lead to significant problems trying to restore a working resolution.

---

5. Set the brightness of the display using the **Brightness** slider.

6. If available (not all Macs support it), check the **Automatically adjust brightness** check box to have your Mac automatically set the brightness based on the ambient light conditions.

7. Move into the open windows and review what you see.

8. If you are comfortable seeing the content of the windows, perform step 4 again but select a higher resolution; if the size of what you see is too small to view comfortably, perform step 4 and select a lower resolution.

9. Repeat steps 4–7 until you've selected the highest resolution at which you can comfortably view what is displayed on the screen.

NOTE: **Multiple Displays**

All Macs support the use of multiple displays. This enables you to either use the multiple screens as one large desktop or show the same image on each display, which is what you typically do when you are using a projector. When multiple displays are connected to your Mac, a Displays pane appears on each so you can configure the resolution and other properties of that display.

Configuring Energy Use

Your Mac doesn't use a lot of power, but still, it's a good idea to minimize its energy use. More importantly, you should configure how a mobile Mac uses energy when you are operating on battery power so you have the longest working time possible between recharges. To set your Mac's energy use, configure the Energy Saver pane (an example is shown in Figure 5.5).

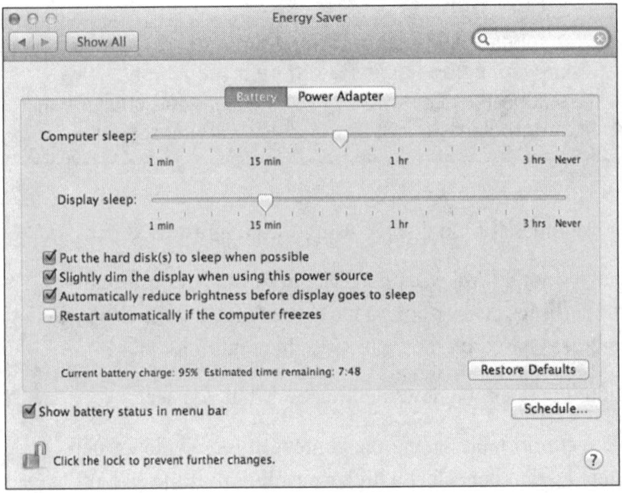

FIGURE 5.5 Use the Energy Saver pane to configure when your Mac and its display sleep to save energy.

When you are using a mobile Mac, the Energy Saver pane has two tabs, which are Battery and Power Adapter. The controls on these tabs are almost the same; click the Battery tab to configure your Mac's energy use while running on battery power and the Power Adapter tab to adjust the settings when your Mac is plugged into electrical power. Use Table 5.3 as a guide to configure these controls.

TABLE 5.3 Energy Saver Preferences

Control	What It Does
Computer sleep slider	Determines the amount of idle time (when you aren't actively using your Mac) that passes before your Mac goes to sleep. In Sleep mode, your Mac uses very little power. You want to set a good balance between saving energy and interrupting your work by putting the Mac to sleep frequently. To wake a sleeping Mac, you can move the mouse, touch the trackpad, press a key, or open its lid (mobile Macs).
Display sleep slider	Determines the amount of idle time that passes before your display goes to sleep. Typically, you should set this to a relatively low amount of time, especially if you are configuring a mobile Mac's Battery settings because the display is a major user of power. To activate the display, move the mouse, touch a key, or touch the trackpad.
Put the hard disk(s) to sleep when possible	This check box causes the hard drives to spin down so they aren't using much power when you aren't actively using them.
Slightly dim the display when using this power source (Battery tab only)	This check box causes your Mac's display to be slightly dimmer than its Brightness setting when you are running a mobile Mac on battery power.
Wake for network access (Power Adapter only)	This check box causes your Mac to wake up when information flows from the network to it, such as another computer accessing its files.
Automatically reduce brightness before display goes to sleep	When this is checked, your display dims right before it goes to sleep. This provides you with a visual warning that the display is about to go dark.

TABLE 5.3   Energy Saver Preferences

Control	What It Does
Restart automatically if the computer freezes	If Mac OS X locks up and isn't working, this setting causes the computer to automatically restart.
Show battery status in menu bar	This check box places the Battery menu on the menu bar; this menu shows the status of the battery's charge or the status of the charging process. Open the menu to see its commands, which include how information is displayed on the menu.

Sometimes when you change settings such that your Mac uses more power than the defaults, you see a warning prompt. Click **OK** to clear the prompt.

To return the settings to what Apple considers optimum, click the **Restore Defaults** button.

> TIP: **Schedule**
>
> If you click the Schedule button, you set a time at which your Mac automatically starts if it is powered off or wakes it if is in Sleep mode. You can also set a time at which it automatically sleeps, restarts, or shuts down. For example, if you never use your Mac between the hours of 11 p.m. and 4 a.m., you can have it shut down at 11 p.m. and start up at 4 a.m. By default, your Mac restores all the windows that were open when it shuts down so you return to the same condition the next time you use your Mac.

Configuring Sounds

Sound is an important part of using a Mac; use the Sound pane to configure your Mac's audio settings. As shown in Figure 5.6, the pane has three tabs and controls at the bottom, which are explained in the following paragraphs.

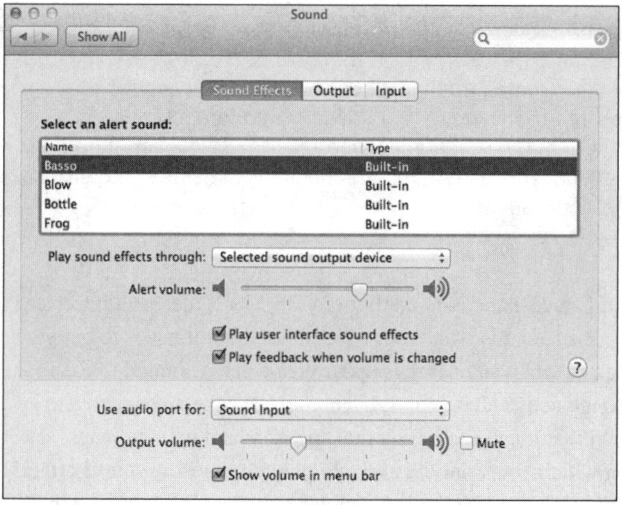

FIGURE 5.6 Use the Sound Effects tab to determine which sounds your Mac uses to get your attention.

Along the bottom of the pane are the general audio controls:

▶ **Use audio port for**. If your Mac has a combined Audio In/Audio Out port, this menu appears. Use it to determine whether the port is used for outgoing or incoming sound.

▶ **Output volume**. This slider sets the overall (also known as the system) volume level.

▶ **Mute**. Check this check box to mute all your Mac's sounds.

▶ **Show volume in menu bar**. When checked, the volume menu, which is the speaker icon, appears on the menu bar. You can use the slider to set the system volume level (it does the same thing as the Output volume slider).

NOTE: **System and Relative Volumes**

The system volume determines a baseline volume level for all sounds emanating from your Mac. Many applications, such as iTunes, also have a volume slider that sets the relative level for that application. When you change the level of the system volume, it changes the volume for all applications. When you change an application's relative volume, only sound from the application is changed. Try to set the system volume at a "mid" level and then use applications' volume controls to change volumes as you are using those applications.

On the Sound Effects pane, you configure your Mac's alert and interface sounds. (An alert sound is what your Mac plays when it needs to get your attention, such as when an error has occurred.) Click a sound to hear it; it also becomes the active alert sound. If you have speakers connected to your Mac such that it can use its internal speakers and external ones, select the device on which you want the alerts to play on the **Play sound effects through** menu. Use the **Alert volume** slider to determine how loud the sound plays. Use the two **Play** check boxes to determine whether interface sounds (such as a sound when you empty the trash) are played or whether you hear feedback when you change your Mac's volume.

Use the Output tab to configure sound coming out of your Mac. If you have more than one output source, such as external speakers, click the speakers you want to use. Controls for the selected speakers appear in the middle of the pane; for example, when you are using the internal speakers on a mobile Mac, you can use the **Balance** slider to set the balance level between the two speakers.

On the Input tab, you can configure how sound goes into your Mac. Select the sound input device you want to use, such as **Internal microphone**. Then, set the level at which sound is captured using the **Input volume** slider and gauge. Check the **Use ambient noise reduction** check box to have your Mac try to filter out extraneous background noise.

TIP: **Volume Buttons**
Mobile Macs and Apple Wireless Keyboards have function buttons that are programmed to control volume. Press F10 to mute your Mac. Press F11 to lower the volume or F12 to increase it. These all change the system volume level.

Setting the Time and Date

It is very important that the time and date be set correctly because all the files with which you work are tagged with this information as are email messages you send and receive. You configure your Mac's clock with the Date & Time pane. It has three tabs: Date & Time, Time Zone, and Clock.

On the Date & Time tab, you can manually set the date and time, but it is better if you let your Mac set these automatically by connecting to a time server. To configure this, check the **Set date and time automatically** check box and then use the menu to select a time server based on your location (such as Apple Americas/U.S. if that happens to be where you are).

On the Time Zone tab, you set where you are located so your Mac can adjust the time according to your current zone. Like time and date, it is more convenient if your have the Mac determine your time zone automatically; check the **Set time zone automatically using current location** check box and your Mac attempts to locate you using a Wi-Fi network. Your current location is indicated with a red dot and your time zone is shown in the light band, as demonstrated in Figure 5.7. To manually configure your time zone, uncheck the check box and click on the map. Then select the closest city on the **Closest City** menu.

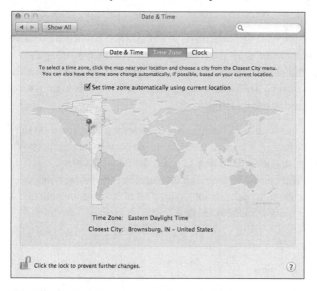

FIGURE 5.7   This Mac is currently located in Brownsburg, Indiana (pushpin) and the Eastern Daylight Time time zone (band).

Use the controls on the Clock tab to configure if and how the time and date are displayed on the menu bar. Check the **Show date and time in menu bar** check box to have this information appear. Then, use the related radio button and check boxes to configure it. For example, check the **Display time with seconds** check box if you want seconds to be shown. To have your Mac announce the time, check the **Announce the time** check box and select how often it is announced on the menu. Use the **Customize Voice** button to select the voice the Mac uses.

Organizing the Launchpad

In Lesson 2, you learned how to use the Launchpad. Here, you learn how to organize the Launchpad by placing its icons where you want them to be and creating folders and placing applications within those folders.

To change the location of icons on the Launchpad, open it and drag the icon you want to move. You can change its location on the current page or drag it off the screen to the left or right to move it to another page (you have to linger at the edge of the screen until the page changes). As you move one icon between other icons, the icons shift to make room for the icon you are moving. When the icon is over its final location, release it.

To create a new folder, drag one icon on top of another. Launchpad creates a new folder and tries to name the folder according to the type of applications you placed together. The folder opens and you see the icons currently stored there. To change the folder's name, select it. When it is highlighted, type its new name, as shown in Figure 5.8.

You can place icons within existing folders by dragging their icons on top of the folder in which you want to place them. You can reorganize icons within folders by dragging them around when the folder is open. To remove an icon from a folder, drag its icon outside of the folder window until the folder closes. To delete a folder, drag all of its icons outside of the folder; when only one icon is left, the folder disappears.

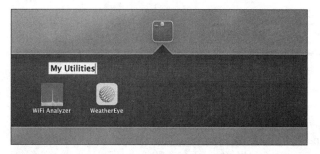

FIGURE 5.8 You can place icons within folders on the Launchpad and change their default names.

Configuring Mission Control

Is Lesson 2, you learned how to use Mission Control to manage the windows on your desktop by switching between desktops, jumping into windows, and so on. In this section, you learn how to configure Mission Control. You do this in two ways. First, configure the Mission Control preferences. Second, configure the desktops you want to use.

Setting Mission Control Preferences

Open the Mission Control pane, as shown in Figure 5.9. Table 5.4 describes the controls you see.

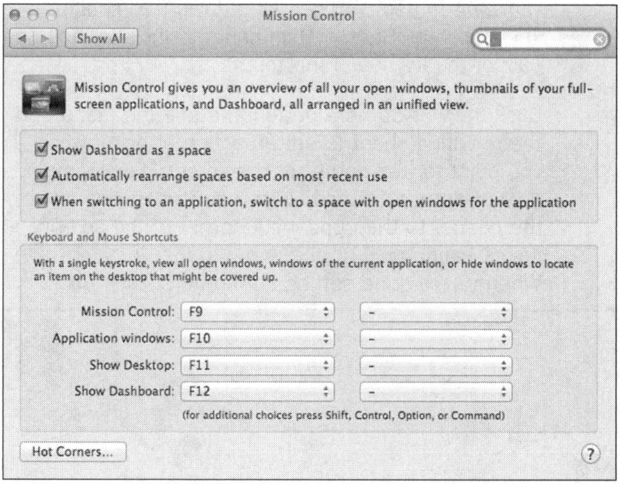

FIGURE 5.9 Use the Mission Control pane to set up Mission Control, Exposé, and the Dashboard.

TABLE 5.4   Mission Control Preferences

Control	What It Does
Show Dashboard as a space	Check the **Show Dashboard as a space** check box if you want the Dashboard to be accessible via its thumbnail when you activate Mission Control.
Automatically rearrange spaces based on most recent use	When this is checked, Mac OS X rearranges your spaces as you move into spaces, close desktops, add new ones, and so on.
When switching to an application, switch to a space with open windows for the application	With this check box checked, when you change applications, such as by using the Application Switcher, you automatically move into the desktop in which that application has windows open.
Keyboard and Mouse Shortcuts	The menus on the left set key combinations (the defaults are F9, F10, F11, and F12) you use to activate Mission Control, show all the windows open in an application, move all the windows off to the sides of the desktop, and show the Dashboard. Use the menus on the right to set mouse clicks for these actions. On the menu for the action you want to configure, choose the keyboard shortcut or mouse click you want to use. You can hold down the modifier keys (such as Shift or Command) to include those as part of the keyboard shortcut.
Hot Corners	Click the Hot Corners button and use the menus on the resulting sheet to set an action to occur when you point to that corner of the screen. For example, if you want the Launchpad to open when you move the pointer to the upper-right corner of the screen, select **Launchpad** on the menu in that location. When you're done setting hot corners, click **OK**.

NOTE: **Spaces**

The term *space* is a general reference to the thumbnails you see in Mission Control. A desktop is a specific kind of space, that being a collection of application windows. The Dashboard is a space as is any application open in Full Screen mode.

TIP: **Function Keys for Exposé**

On Mobile Macs and Apple Wireless Keyboards, you hold down the fn key and press the related default keyboard shortcut to activate Mission Control functions (if you don't hold down this key, you perform the preprogrammed function, such as changing volume, instead).

Setting Up Desktops

As you saw in Lesson 2, Mission Control enables you to use desktops, which are collections of applications that you group together. The value of using desktops is that, via Mission Control, you can easily jump between applications, each of which can have multiple windows open. And as you saw, Mission Control also enables you to access the Dashboard along with applications that are open in Full Screen mode.

You first create a desktop and then add the applications you want to include in that space. Here's how:

1. Open Mission Control. The Dashboard (if included), current desktops, and applications in full screen mode are shown at the top of the screen (see Figure 5.10). The applications and windows open in the current desktop are shown in the center of the screen.

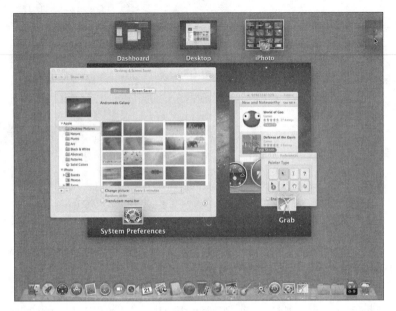

FIGURE 5.10   Click the Add button (+) to create a new desktop.

2. Point to the upper-right corner of the screen until the **Add Space** button (+) appears; when it does, click it. A new space titled Desktop *X*, where *X* is a sequential number, appears.

3. Click in the new desktop as shown in Figure 5.11. It becomes active and is ready for you to configure.

4. To add an application to the space, perform a secondary click on its Dock icon, and on the resulting menu select Options and one of the following choices:

   ▶ **All Desktops**. This adds the application to all desktops so it is available no matter what desktop you are using.

   ▶ **This Desktop**. This adds the application to the current desktop.

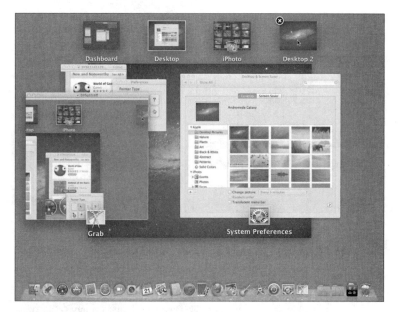

FIGURE 5.11   Click a new desktop to move into and configure it.

▶ **None**. This removes the application from all desktops so it
behaves independently of the desktop you are using.

NOTE: **Already Assigned?**

If an application is already assigned to a desktop, you see Desktop
X, where *X* is the number of the desktop to which it is assigned.
You can reassign the application using the other commands or
leave it where it is.

TIP: **No Dock Icon?**

If the icon for the application you want to add to a desktop isn't on
the Dock, launch the application. When it opens, its icon appears
on the Dock.

5. Repeat steps 1–4 until you've configured all the desktops you want to use.

6. To remove a space you no longer need, open Mission Control, point to the space, and click the **Remove Space** button (x). The space is deleted; any applications in that space are set to All Desktops.

TIP: **Desktop Pictures and Spaces**

Each desktop can have its own desktop picture. Move into a desktop and set its desktop picture. Change to the next desktop and repeat. Using a different picture for each desktop makes it easier to tell which one you are in and makes your desktop even more fun.

Configuring the Dashboard

In Lesson 2, you learned how to use the Dashboard and the widgets it contains. In this section, you learn how to configure the Dashboard to make it as useful as it can be. Open the Dashboard, and do any or all of the following:

▶ **Change widget locations**. To change the location of a widget on the Dashboard, simply drag it to where you want it to appear.

▶ **Configure widgets**. Most widgets allow some configuration. For example, if the widget is location based, you can set the location you want to use. To configure a widget, hover over it and look for the *i* button; when it appears, click it. The widget moves into configuration mode. Use the configuration tools. When you're finished, click **Done** to save your changes. The widget operates according to the configuration you set.

▶ **Add widgets**. To add a widget that is installed on your Mac to your Dashboard, open the Dashboard and click the Add button (+) in the lower-left corner of the Dashboard. The available widgets appear on the toolbar at the bottom of the screen. You can browse the widgets by clicking the arrow buttons on each end. To add a widget to your Dashboard, drag the widget from the toolbar onto your Dashboard. You can place it anywhere on your Dashboard. Then, configure the widget you added.

▶ **Remove widgets**. To remove widgets from the Dashboard, open the widget toolbar by clicking the Add button (+). To remove a widget, click its remove button (x) located in the upper-left corner of the widget you want to remove. You can add the widgets again if you want to.

▶ **Install new widgets**. You can download and install new widgets from the Internet. To do this, open the widget toolbar and click the Manage Widgets button. In the Manage Widgets window, click **More Widgets**. Your Web browser opens and you move to the Dashboard widgets page. Browse for widgets in which you are interested. To download a widget, click its **Download** button. Click **Install** at the prompt. The widget is downloaded and installed on your Dashboard.

TIP: **One Widget Many Widgets**

You can add multiple instances of the same widget to your Dashboard. For example, you might want to show the weather in multiple locations; add a widget and configure it for one location; add it again, set a different location, and so on.

Summary

In this lesson you learned how to personalize Mac OS X Lion. In the next lesson, you learn how to connect to the Internet and local networks.

LESSON 6

Connecting Your Mac to the Internet and a Local Network

In this lesson, you learn how to connect your Mac to the Internet and a local network. You also learn how to use services on a local network, including file sharing.

Connecting Your Mac to the Internet

To get the most from your Mac running Mac OS X Lion, it needs to be connected to the Internet so you can email, browse the Web, download files, and so on. There are two basic ways to connect, and you'll probably use both of them at various times.

You should create a local network (also known as a local area network, or LAN) to not only connect your Mac to the Internet, but also to enable you to connect multiple computers and other devices to the Net and to be able to use Mac OS X's great network features, such as file sharing, among those computers.

You also might need to connect to "someone else's" network, such as Wi-Fi networks in public places, including airports, coffee shops, hotels, schools, and so on. Connecting to these is easy because all Macs include Wi-Fi networking capabilities. All you have to do is select and connect to a network; sometimes it's free but other times you have to pay a fee and obtain an account.

Installing and Configuring a Local Network with Internet Connection

There are many ways to create a local network that employ various kinds of hardware and software. However, one of the best and easiest ways to build a local network for Macs and other devices is based on an Apple Airport Extreme Base Station or Time Capsule. This hardware has lots of capabilities that provide everything you need for a small, local network. And, the software you need to create and manage these devices is built in to Mac OS X Lion. Therefore, this approach is the focus of this lesson. The local network described in this lesson includes the following components:

▶ **DSL or Cable Modem**. Your network requires a connection to the Internet, which in most cases comes through either digital subscriber line (DSL) or cable. Both options include a modem that delivers the connection to your location. The modem is connected to either a phone line or cable and connects to the base station with an Ethernet cable. The modem provides the connection to the Internet that enables you to access your Internet account.

NOTE: **Internet Account Assumed**

This lesson assumes you already have an Internet connection provided by an Internet service provider (ISP) over a DSL or cable connection. It also assumes the required modem is installed and configured. If this isn't the case for you, you need to get this done before this lesson will be of much help to you. The best way to start is to contact your cable provider and obtain Internet service (which includes installation of a cable modem or the provision of a self-install kit). Another great option is to find a DSL ISP; check with your local telephone company or other Internet service providers to get information about your options. When you get an account, you will have a DSL modem installed or receive a self-install kit. Be sure to explore all your options to make sure you get the fastest account possible at the best price.

▶ **Apple Extreme Base Station or Time Capsule**. These devices connect to the DSL or cable modem and do two primary things. The first is to provide a wired and wireless network to which you

connect to gain access to the Internet and communicate with the
other devices on the networks. The second is to manage the traffic flow across the networks and protect your networks from
attacks coming from the Internet. Both Apple Extreme Base
Station and Time Capsule offer high-speed wireless performance
and multiple Ethernet ports to which you can connect devices to
add them to your network. You can use Mac OS X's AirPort
Utility to configure and manage both types. The only difference
between them is that the Time Capsule, as shown in Figure 6.1,
also includes a hard drive to which you can back up data—a very
handy feature indeed. Because the purpose of this lesson is creating a network, from here on, both devices are referred to as a
base station because they function identically for that purpose.

FIGURE 6.1 An Apple Time Capsule provides a local network and includes
a hard disk you can use to back up your Mac.

▶ **Apple Express Base Stations (optional).** These base stations,
shown in Figure 6.2, are useful for many purposes, two of which
are to extend the range of your wireless network should the base
station's range not be sufficient to cover the desired area and to
be able to stream iTunes music to different locations. Although
adding and configuring these base stations are outside the scope

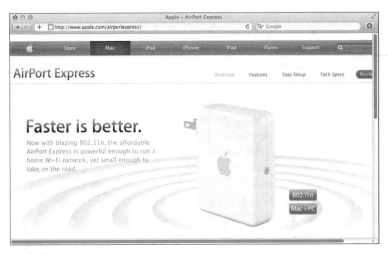

FIGURE 6.2 AirPort Express Base Stations enable you to expand the coverage of a wireless network and stream iTunes content.

of this lesson, you should be aware of them in case you need to add one or more to your network.

NOTE: **AirPort Express for Travelers**

An AirPort Express can be a nice addition to a traveler's toolkit. That's because you can use one to create your own wireless network to which you can easily connect multiple devices, such as a Mac and an iPhone. All you have to do is connect the Ethernet port on the base station to an active Ethernet port. With a minor bit of configuration, similar to configuring a Time Capsule or AirPort Extreme Base Station, the Express connects to the Internet and provides a wireless network for your devices.

▶ **Ethernet cables**. In most cases, you'll be connecting some devices, such as printers or non-mobile computers, to the network via Ethernet. So, you need the appropriate number and length of cables to make these connections.

▶ **Ethernet hub (optional)**. An Ethernet hub connects to your base station; its function is to provide additional Ethernet ports to which you can connect various devices, should the number of ports on the base station not be sufficient or you want to route a single cable from the base station to a cluster of other devices. In most cases, a simple hub requires no configuration; you connect a LAN Ethernet port on the base station to the input port on the hub and power it up. You can then connect devices to the hub to add them to the network.

▶ **Printers**. Adding printers to a network is a great way to share them among multiple devices. Printers connect to the network via Ethernet, wirelessly, or to the USB port on an AirPort Extreme Base Station or Time Capsule. Once connected, the printer is accessible to any device communicating on the network. Connecting to and configuring printers is covered in the next lesson.

▶ **Macintosh computers**. Of course, you'll want to include at least one Mac on your network, but it's likely you'll have more than one. Macs can connect wirelessly or via Ethernet. Both options are explained later in this lesson.

▶ **Mobile devices**. Wi-Fi–enabled devices, such as iPhones, iPads, and iPod touches, can also connect to the network to access its resources.

> NOTE: **Shameless Self-promotion**
>
> If you have an iPhone or iPod touch, check out my books *My iPhone* and *My iPod touch*.

▶ **Windows computers.**Windows computers and Macs share the same networking technologies so you can also connect Windows PCs to your network to enable them to access the network's resources.

Installing and configuring a base station and the associated components like that shown in Figure 6.3 is outside the scope of this lesson, but here's a quick overview of the steps:

1. **Install and configure the modem.** This is often done by the ISP, but some ISPs send you a self-install kit.

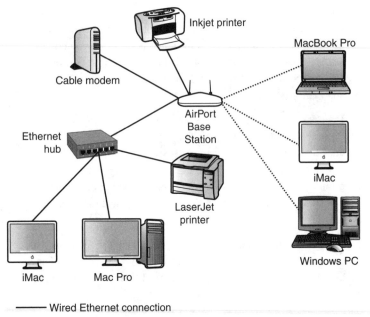

FIGURE 6.3 A local network like this one isn't difficult to set up and is very useful.

CAUTION: **No ISP Software, Please**

If your ISP installs and configures your modem for you, don't allow the installer to install any software on your Mac. It's not needed to connect to the Internet because your Mac already has all it needs to connect to the Internet. The software installed by ISPs minimally wastes disk space with files you don't need, but often includes tools to help the ISP generate revenue, such as driving you to the ISP's home page.

---

2. **Install and configure the base station**. You connect the base station's wide area network (WAN) port to the modem's output port via an Ethernet cable. Then use the AirPort Utility applica-

tion, located in the Utilities folder within the Applications folder, to configure the base station. This includes connecting it to the Internet, creating a wireless network, and so on. Using the AirPort Utility is fairly straightforward, especially for new base stations because the software's assistant guides you through the process.

3. **Connect an Ethernet hub**. If you will be using an Ethernet hub, connect its input port to one of the available Ethernet ports on the base station. Then, power up the hub.

4. **Connect Ethernet devices**. Using an Ethernet cable, connect devices (such as Macs, Windows PCs, printers, and so on) to the wired part of the network, via a port on the base station or on the hub. Connecting and configuring a Mac via Ethernet is covered later in this lesson.

NOTE: **Connecting Devices**

Connecting devices to a network, via Ethernet or wirelessly, consists of two tasks. The first is to make the connection over which the device will communicate with the network; this will be either via an Ethernet cable or wirelessly. The second is to configure the device to communicate over the network. Sometimes these two tasks happen simultaneously, such as when you connect a Mac to a Wi-Fi network. In other situations, these are two distinct steps, such as when you connect your Mac to an Ethernet network.

---

5. **Connect wireless devices**. Connect wireless devices to the wireless network being provided by the base station. Connecting Macs to wireless networks is covered later in this lesson.

TIP: **One at a Time**

When you are connecting devices to a network, it's a good idea to connect and configure each device and make sure it is working as expected before moving to the next device. Sometimes, connecting multiple devices at the same time can be confusing and occasionally cause a problem. Keep things as simple as possible to make building a network go more smoothly.

Connecting Your Mac to a Local Network

After the modem, base station, and Ethernet hub (if applicable) are up and running, you can connect your Mac to the network via Ethernet or Wi-Fi. Both tasks are straightforward.

Connecting Your Mac to a Network Using Ethernet

To connect your Mac to an Ethernet network, perform the following steps:

1. Connect an Ethernet cable to your Mac and to the base station or hub.

2. Open the System Preferences application.

3. Click **Network**.

4. Authenticate yourself by clicking the **Lock** icon, entering your Administrator password, and clicking **Unlock**.

5. Select the Ethernet connection. The Ethernet tools appear in the right pane of the window. The Ethernet connection's status should be Connected. If not, there is a problem with the network. You need to ensure the device to which the Mac is connecting is powered up and functioning correctly.

6. On the Configure IPv4 menu, choose **Using DHCP**.

7. Click **Apply.** Your Mac communicates with the base station, and the base station assigns an IP address to it as shown in Figure 6.4. This indicates the Mac is connected to the network and, assuming the base station has a working Internet connection, is connected to the Internet.

> NOTE: **Most Common Configuration**
>
> This lesson describes the most common type of network configuration for a home or small business. There are many other possibilities, such as using a predetermined Internet Protocol (IP) address instead of using Dynamic Host Configuration Protocol (DHCP). Regardless of how your base station is configured for its Internet

connection, which is determined by the specific account you have, in almost all cases, your devices connect via DHCP. This is good because the base station manages each device's IP address for you automatically.

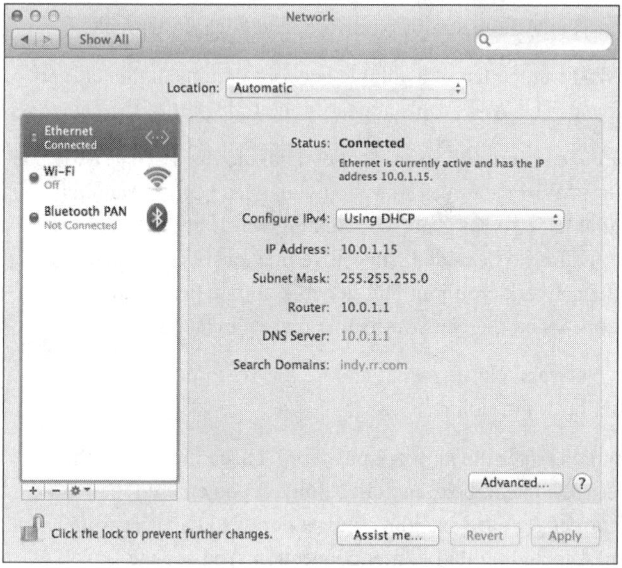

FIGURE 6.4 This Mac is connected to the Internet via Ethernet.

CAUTION: **Internet Attacks**

You should ensure your base station is providing Network Address Translation (NAT) services. This means it shields the addresses of devices connected to the network from exposure to the Internet; the only address exposed is for the base station. NAT is an effective means of protecting your Mac from attacks coming from the Internet. If you ever connect your Mac directly to the modem, make sure its firewall is operating before you do so; you should also run the firewall even if your Mac is connected only to the base station. See Lesson 10, "Securing and Protecting Your Mac," for more information about protecting your Mac.

Connecting Your Mac to a Network Using Wi-Fi

To connect your Mac to the network wirelessly, perform the following steps:

1. Open the Network pane of the System Preferences application.

2. If necessary, authenticate yourself by clicking the **Lock** icon, entering your Administrator password, and clicking **Unlock**.

3. Click **Wi-Fi** in the list of available network options in the left part of the pane. The Wi-Fi tools appear in the right part of the pane.

4. If Wi-Fi is currently off, turn it on by clicking the **Turn Wi-Fi On** button. Wi-Fi services start, and your Mac begins scanning for available networks (you see radiating waves at the top of the Wi-Fi menu if it is enabled). If you've previously connected to an available network, you join that network automatically and its name appears on the Network Name pop-up menu.

5. On the **Network Name** menu, choose the Wi-Fi network your base station is providing.

6. If prompted, enter the network password, check the **Remember this network** check box, and click **Join.** If you entered the password correctly, your Mac joins the network and can access its resources, including its Internet connection. You see the Connected status message and the Mac's IP address as shown in Figure 6.5.

7. If you want to be prompted to join new networks, check the **Ask to join new networks** check box. With this enabled, when you move your Mac into an area with networks you've not connected to previously, you're prompted to connect to those networks.

8. Check the **Show Wi-Fi status in menu bar** check box to put the Wi-Fi menu on your menu bar. You can use this menu to quickly select and control your Wi-Fi connection.

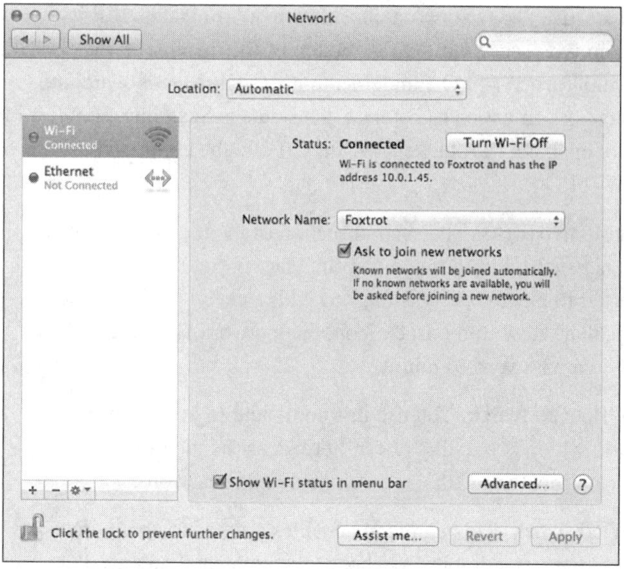

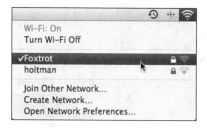

FIGURE 6.5   This Mac has a Wi-Fi connection to the network.

To manage your wireless network connections, open the Wi-Fi menu (see Figure 6.6).

FIGURE 6.6   The Wi-Fi menu makes managing your wireless connections easy.

The Wi-Fi menu contains the following:

▶ **Signal strength of the current network**. When you are connected to a wireless network, it is marked with a check mark and the number of dark waves at the top of the menu indicates the strength of the signal.

▶ **Wi-Fi status**. The first two items relate to Wi-Fi status. If it is turned on, you see Wi-Fi: On at the top of the menu with the command Turn Wi-Fi Off underneath it. If your Mac is searching for a network to which to connect, the status is Scanning. If Wi-Fi is not enabled, the status is Wi-Fi: Off and the command is Turn Wi-Fi On.

▶ **Available networks**. The second section of the menu shows you all the networks within range of your Mac. If you are currently connected to a network, it is marked with a check mark. If a network is marked with the Lock icon, that network is secure and you need a password to join it.

▶ **Join Other Network**. You use this command to join a closed network, which is one that doesn't broadcast its identity and for which you must know the network name and password.

▶ **Create Network**. This command enables you to set up a wireless network between computers. Choose the command and use the resulting dialog box to create a wireless network. Other computers can use the network that you create to share files, play network games, and access other services you want to provide.

▶ **Open Network Preferences**. This command opens the Network pane of the System Preferences application.

Connecting to Public Wi-Fi Networks

Connecting to Public Wi-Fi networks is actually quite similar to using Wi-Fi to connect to your LAN. Here's how to do it:

1. Open the **Wi-Fi** menu.

2. Wait a moment or two for your Mac to scan the area for available networks. You see the networks available to you.

3. Select the **network** you want to join.

4. If prompted, enter the network's password and click **Join.** For most public networks, you don't need a password to join the network, but you do need to sign in to be able to access its resources, including an Internet connection.

5. Open Safari by clicking its icon on the Dock. The Safari web browser opens and moves to your home page or to the provider's login page. If you move to your home page, skip the rest of these steps. In most cases, you need to at least agree to terms and conditions before you can access the Internet. In others, you need to watch an ad to be able to access the Internet. Or, you might have to obtain a temporary account to be able to do so.

6. Follow the onscreen prompts to be able to access the Internet. For example, if you have to watch an ad to obtain access, do so. If you have to have an account, you need to sign in to an existing account or sign up for a temporary account, which involves a fee (typically depending on how long you want to access the account).

> TIP: **Skip the Ads**
>
> In many cases, a link that is something like, "If the video doesn't play, click here" appears along with the ad. You can usually skip the ad just by clicking this link even if the ad does play correctly.

Working on a Local Network

Connecting to the Internet is just one of the useful things you can do with a local network. You might find some of the following capabilities almost as useful as Internet access:

- ▶ File sharing with AirDrop
- ▶ Sharing content in applications
- ▶ Sharing screens

Sharing Files with AirDrop

AirDrop makes copying files to other people's Macs (running Mac OS X Lion or later) simple. That's because you don't need to do any configuration—your Mac automatically identifies any other Lion users with which your Mac can communicate via Wi-Fi; the Macs don't need to be on the same network, but they do have to have Wi-Fi turned on. You can copy a file to another person just by dragging it onto his icon. Likewise, someone can copy a file to your Mac by dragging it onto your icon.

To send a file to someone else, do the following:

1. Open a Finder window and click **AirDrop** on the Sidebar. Your Mac locates any other Macs with which it can communicate via Wi-Fi running Mac OS X Lion (or later) and that have an AirDrop window open and presents an icon for each.

2. Open another Finder window and move to the file you want to share.

3. Drag the file from the second window and drop it onto the person's icon with whom you want to share the file, as shown in Figure 6.7.

FIGURE 6.7 Sharing a file with AirDrop is as simple as dragging a file onto someone's icon.

4. In the resulting prompt, click **Send.** The file is sent to that person. If he accepts the file, it is copied to his computer. If not, you see a message telling you the file was rejected; click **OK** to clear the message.

When someone AirDrops a file to you, you see a prompt on your screen as shown in Figure 6.8. Click one of the following options:

▶ **Save**. The file is saved in your Downloads folder in your Home folder.

▶ **Save and Open**. The file is saved in your Downloads folder and opens in the associated application.

▶ **Decline**. The file isn't copied, and the sender receives a message stating you've declined the file.

FIGURE 6.8   This prompt indicates someone wants to share a file with you.

Finder window and minimize that window on the Dock. That way, your AirDrop is always available to others and you won't be taking up valuable desktop space with its window. If someone sends you a file, the AirDrop window and prompt jump onto your desktop automatically.

Sharing Content in Applications

Many applications enable you to share content with other people on your network. iTunes enables you to allow other iTunes users to access the content in your iTunes Library on their computers; likewise, using iPhoto, you can allow others to view your photos and even import them into their own iPhoto libraries. How this works varies from application to application, but a quick example using iTunes gives you the idea.

To share your content, configure the application using its Preferences:

1. Open Preferences and click the Sharing tab as shown in Figure 6.9.

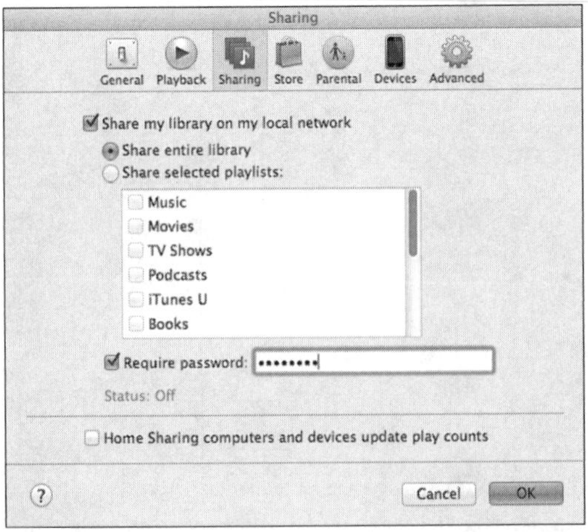

FIGURE 6.9 You can share your iTunes music and video with other people on your network.

2. Check the **Share my library on my local network** check box.

3. Click **Share entire library** or click **Share selected playlists** and check the check box for each playlist you want to share.

4. To require people to enter a password before accessing your content, check the **Require password** check box and enter the password in the box.

5. Click **OK**. Your content becomes available on the network.

To access your content, the person selects the shared resources in the same application on his computer.

Sharing Screens

Sharing screens enables you to control a Mac on your network as if you are sitting in front of it.

To allow screen sharing, configure it on the Mac whose screen you want to share by performing the following steps:

1. Open the Sharing pane of the System Preferences application.

2. Click the **Screen Sharing** service on the service list. The controls for screen sharing appear.

3. Click **Computer Settings.** The Computer Settings sheet appears.

4. Click the **Anyone may request permission to control screen** check box.

5. Click **OK.** The sheet closes.

6. Click the **All users** radio button.

7. Click the **On** check box for Screen Sharing. Screen sharing services start, and the Mac is available to users on your local network. The Screen Sharing status becomes On, as shown in Figure 6.10.

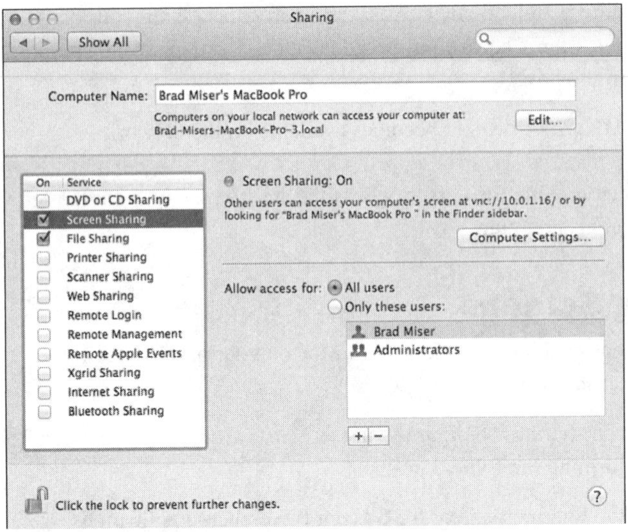

FIGURE 6.10 This Mac is configured to allow others to request to share its screen.

To share the Mac's screen, do the following:

1. Open a Finder window.

2. On the Sidebar, select the **Mac** whose screen you want to share.

3. Click Share Screen as shown in Figure 6.11.

4. Click **Ask to share the display.** If the person using the Mac accepts your request, the Screen Sharing application opens. The other Mac's desktop appears within the Screen Sharing window on your Mac as shown in Figure 6.12.

The Screen Sharing window, which has the name of the Mac whose screen you are sharing as its title, contains the desktop of the Mac whose screen you are sharing, including open Finder windows, applications, and documents. When your cursor is inside the Screen Sharing application window, any action you take is done on the Mac whose screen you are sharing. When you move outside the window, the cursor for your Mac separates from the shared Mac's cursor and the shared Mac's cursor freezes (unless, of course, the user at that Mac is doing something, in which case you see the results of her actions).

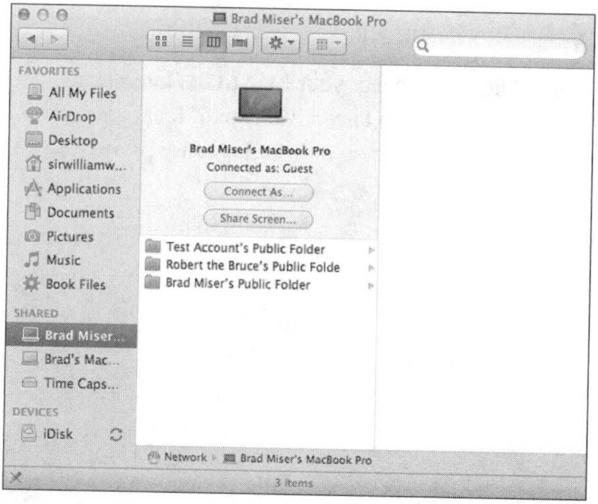

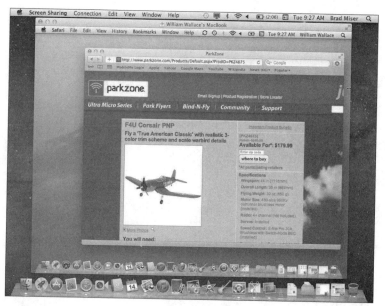

FIGURE 6.11   Select a Mac and click Share Screen to access that Mac over the network.

FIGURE 6.12   In the Screen Sharing application window, you see the desktop of the Mac being shared.

Summary

In this lesson you learned how to connect your Mac to the Internet and a local network; you also learned how to take advantage of local network services. In the next lesson, you learn how to install and use printers.

LESSON 7

Installing and Using Printers

In this lesson, you learn how to configure and use printers.

Understanding Printing Options

Printing is an important capability for almost any Mac user. Fortunately, Mac OS X Lion supports many kinds of printers, and the tools you use to install and work with printers are both powerful and easy to use.

Understanding Printer Types

Most Mac users use either inkjet or laser printers.

Inkjet printers produce excellent quality text and good-to-excellent quality graphics. For personal printers or those shared by only a few people, inkjets are hard to beat. Quality inkjet printers are inexpensive. Support for many Hewlett-Packard, Lexmark, Epson, and other inkjet printers is built in to Mac OS X.

Laser printers produce superb quality for both text and graphics. They are also very fast and are the best choice for network printing. Black-only laser printers are inexpensive, but color laser printers can be a bit pricey. Though more expensive than inkjet printers, laser printers are also quite affordable, especially if you get a refurbished model.

A factor to consider when selecting a printer is that inkjets use a lot of ink and cartridges are expensive. If you do a lot of printing, a laser printer can be a less expensive option in the long run when you consider the cost of the consumable supplies (ink versus toner). Or, you might consider a laser printer for black-and-white printing and an inkjet for color printing.

Understanding Printer Connection Options

There are three ways you can connect a printer to your Mac: directly through USB or Ethernet, through a wired or wireless network, or through a direct wireless connection.

To connect a printer directly to your Mac, you simply attach the printer cable to the appropriate port on your Mac (USB or Ethernet).

How you connect a printer to a network depends on the type of network you are using. If you are using an Ethernet network, you attach a cable from the nearest hub to your printer. If your network includes an Apple base station, you can connect a printer to the base station's USB or Ethernet port to share that printer on the network.

Some printers support a direct wireless connection with a Mac, through Wi-Fi or Bluetooth. How you connect this type of printer depends on the specific model. The other two connection options are much more common. If you choose a printer that supports a direct wireless connection, refer to its documentation for help installing and configuring it.

Understanding Printer Sharing

Mac OS X Lion supports printer sharing. This enables you to share a printer connected directly to your Mac (or through a network for that matter) with other Macs with which your Mac can communicate. The advantage of this is that you don't need any additional network hardware to be able to access a single printer from multiple Macs. The downside is that the Mac must be turned on and connected to the printer for the printer to be shared.

For that reason, it is generally better to connect a printer to a network to share it among multiple devices, but in this lesson, you learn how to share a printer in case you need to do so.

Understanding PDF

The Portable Document Format (PDF) was created by Adobe as a means to share documents among computers without requiring those computers to have the same applications and fonts. Over time, PDF has become the standard for electronic documents, especially for sharing over email, the Web, and so on.

Mac OS X Lion includes support for PDF documents. You can save a file as a PDF document from any application. You can also view PDF documents using the Preview application.

Installing and Configuring a Printer Connected to a Mac

Connecting a printer directly to a Mac and configuring (or sharing) it is a straightforward operation. There are two required steps and one optional step. First, connect the printer to the Mac. Second, configure the printer. The third, and optional, step is to share the printer with other Macs.

Connect the printer to the Mac's USB or Ethernet port using the required cable.

NOTE: **USB Printer Connections**

It's much more common to use USB to connect a printer to a Mac than Ethernet, but if a printer supports an Ethernet connection, you can use that to connect it to a Mac. Because Macs typically have only one Ethernet port, using it for a printer means you use it to connect the Mac to a network, which is the more typical use of Ethernet ports.

Next, configure the printer by performing the following steps:

1. Open the Print & Scan pane of the System Preferences application.

2. Click the **Add** (+) button.

3. If prompted, choose **Add Other Printer or Scanner**. The Add Printer window displays with the Default tab selected.

4. Select the **printer** you want to configure as shown in Figure 7.1. The printer's name is entered and the driver is selected on the Print Using pop-up menu automatically.

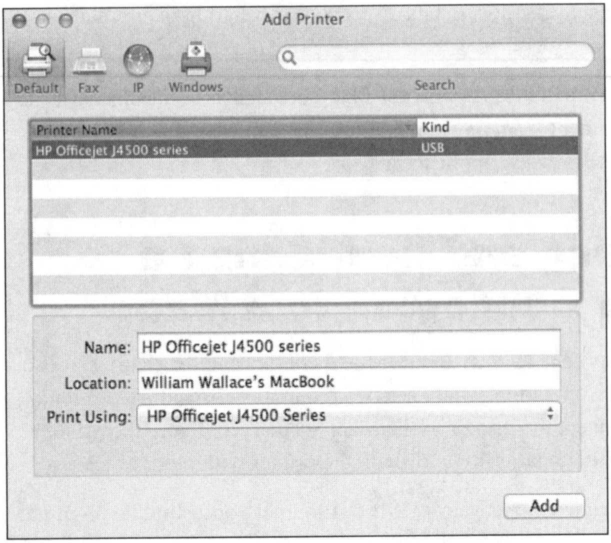

FIGURE 7.1   Lion identifies printers connected to a USB port; select one to configure it.

5. If you want to give the printer a different name, edit the name shown in the Name field. By default, this is the model of printer you selected.

6. Type the location of the printer in the Location field; in most cases, you should leave the default information.

7. Click **Add**. The printer is set up and the Add Printer window closes.

NOTE: **Printer Drivers**

Mac OS X Lion, like all operating systems, requires specific printer driver software to be able to communicate with a printer. In almost all cases, the system already has the driver software and selects it automatically on the Print Using pop-up. If this doesn't happen, open the Print Using menu and select the driver you want to use. If you can't find an appropriate driver, you need to download it from the manufacturer's website and install it on your Mac.

8. If you want the printer to be your default, choose it on the **Default printer** pop-up menu.

9. Choose the default paper size on the **Default paper size** pop-up menu.

Test the printer by printing a document (information about printing is covered later in this lesson). If the print job works correctly, you are done installing and configuring the printer.

If you want to share the printer with other Macs on your network, perform the following steps:

1. Click the **Sharing Preferences** button on the Print & Scan pane. The Sharing pane opens.

2. Check the **Printer Sharing** check box to start printer sharing services.

3. Check the **check box** next to a printer you want to share.

4. Configure the people who have access to the printer using the Users list. By default, the group Everyone has the Can Print permission as shown in Figure 7.2. This means everyone on your network can print to the shared printer. In most cases, this is what you want. However, if you want to limit access to printing, choose No Access on the pop-up menu next to everyone. Then add the people with whom you do want to share the printer and give them Can Print permission. Anyone that is on the same network and who has permission to print to the printer can use it.

Installing and Configuring a Network Printer

Although sharing a printer is useful, it is limited because it depends on the Mac sharing the printer being turned on and connected to the network. It is usually better to share a printer by first connecting a printer to a network and then accessing the printer from any Macs, PCs, or other devices that are also connected to that network.

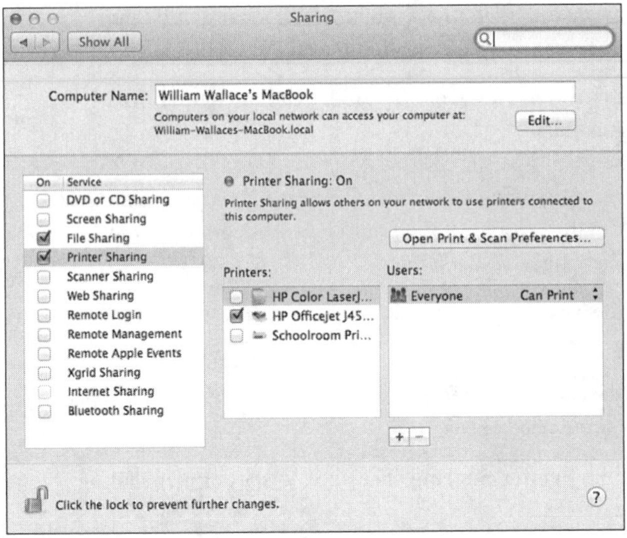

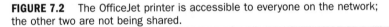

FIGURE 7.2   The OfficeJet printer is accessible to everyone on the network; the other two are not being shared.

First, connect the printer to the network. There are a couple of common ways to do this, which are the following:

▶ Connect the printer to an AirPort base station or other network routing device using its USB port or an Ethernet port.

▶ Connect the printer to an Ethernet port on a hub that is part of the network.

After the printer is connected to the network and is turned on, you can configure a Mac to access it by performing the following steps:

1. Open the Print & Scan pane of the System Preferences application.

2. Click the **Add** (+) button. The printers available on the network are scanned and presented on the drop-down list in the Nearby Printers section as shown in Figure 7.3 or they appear in the Add Printer dialog box as shown in Figure 7.1.

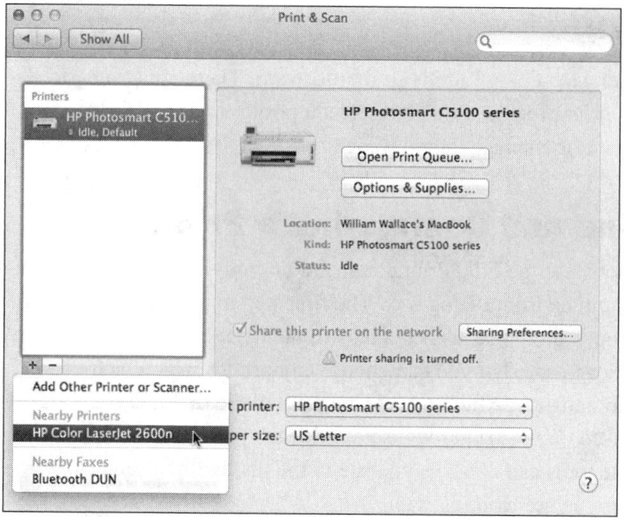

FIGURE 7.3 Lion automatically locates printers on the network.

3. Select the **printer** to which you want to connect. The Set Up sheet for the printer appears. You use this to configure the printer's options. The options you see depend on the capabilities of the printer.

4. Configure the options for the printer.

5. Click **OK**. You return to the System Preferences application and see the printer you selected on the list of printers.

6. If you want the printer to be your default, choose it on the **Default printer** pop-up menu.

7. Choose the default paper size on the **Default paper size** pop-up menu.

Test the printer by printing a document (information about printing appears in the next section). If the print job works correctly, you are done installing and configuring the printer.

Printing

Printing under Mac OS X Lion is straightforward. There are two basic elements of the print process. One is to select a printer and configure the print job. The other is to manage the print job.

Selecting and Configuring a Printer

All applications use the File, Print command or cmd+P to print. This command brings up the Print dialog box. The first step in printing is to select the printer you want to use. This defaults to the default printer selected on the Print & Scan pane, but you can choose any printer with which your Mac can communicate. After you select a printer, the dialog box configures itself based on the printer you selected; each printer has its own options so the tools and controls you see in the dialog box change based on the printer you are working with.

For any printer, the Print dialog box has two modes: one is where the details are hidden, as shown in Figure 7.4, and the other provides access

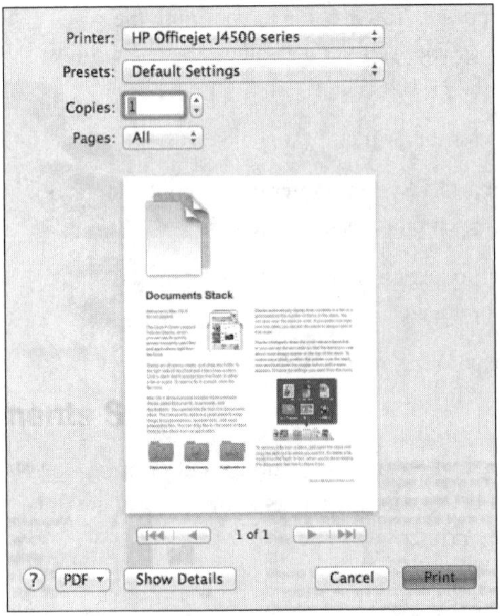

FIGURE 7.4 If you don't need to change the printer's settings, this dialog box is all you need to print documents.

to all the configuration tools for the selected printer, as shown in Figure 7.5. To show or hide the details, click Show Details or Hide Details, respectively.

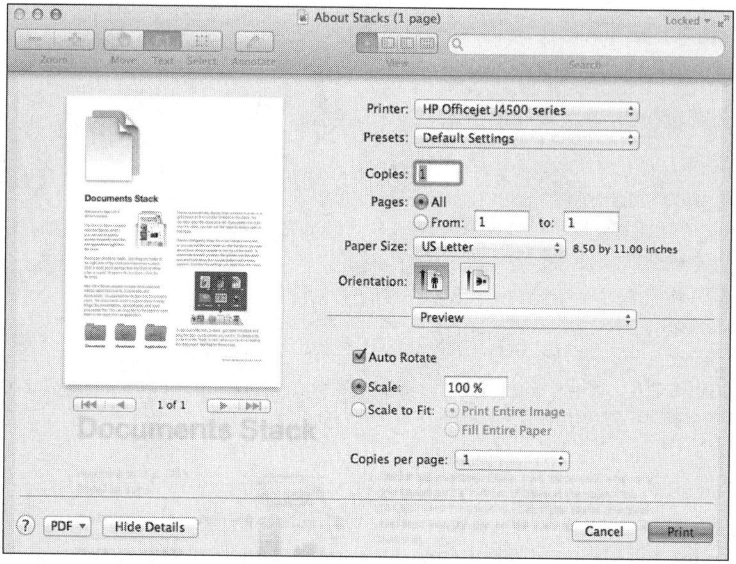

FIGURE 7.5 Showing the details enables you to configure all of a printer's options.

Use the pop-up menus, radio buttons, and boxes on the Print sheet to configure the print job (the menus vary, depending on the type of printer you are using). When you are ready to print, click **Print**.

Managing the Print Process

While documents are printing, you can use the printer's application to manage its print jobs, such as to cancel a document that is printing. As soon as you click the Print button, the print process starts and the printer's application opens, as shown in Figure 7.6.

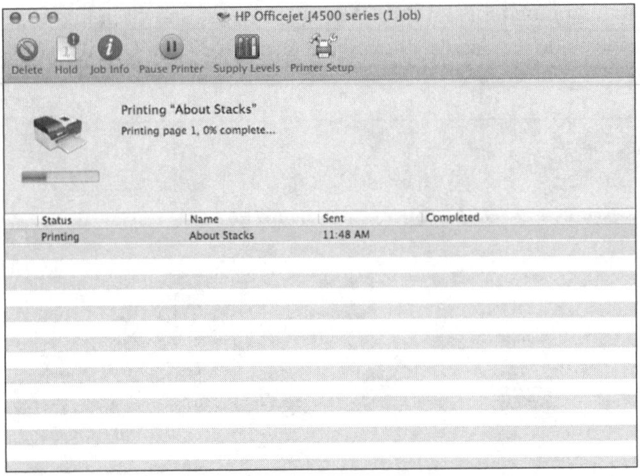

FIGURE 7.6 When you print, the printer's application opens, enabling you to manage its print jobs.

The printer's application shows you the status of the current print jobs; you can use the buttons on its toolbar to delete a job by selecting it from the list and clicking Cancel. You can also place a job on hold, get more information about it, or pause it.

For some applications, you can also determine the status of the printer's ink or toner cartridges by clicking the Supply Levels button. The Printer Setup button enables you to make more advanced configurations of the printer.

When a print job has finished, you can quit the printer's application or just leave it open in the background.

Printing to PDF

Creating a PDF version of a document is a great way to share it via email, over the Web, and so on. That's because a PDF document is self-contained; for example, it doesn't depend on the viewing computer having the same fonts installed on it to retain the document's formatting. All that is needed to view a document is an application capable of opening PDF documents; every computer platform and mobile device has at least one (in most cases, many more than one) free application that can display PDF documents.

Support for PDFs is built in to Mac OS X Lion, so you don't need any additional software to create PDF versions of your documents.

To create a PDF of a document, do the following:

1. Open the document for which you want to create a PDF, and select the **Print** command.

2. Open the **PDF** pop-up menu and select **Save as PDF**. The Save dialog box appears as shown in Figure 7.7.

3. Type a name for the PDF file you are creating and choose a location in which to save it.

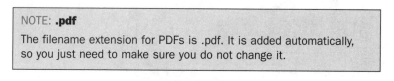

FIGURE 7.7 Use this Save dialog box to create a PDF version of a document.

NOTE: **.pdf**

The filename extension for PDFs is .pdf. It is added automatically, so you just need to make sure you do not change it.

4. Add title, author, and subject information.

5. Create keywords (used during Spotlight and other searches) in the Keywords field. (For information on Spotlight searches, see Lesson 2, "Working on the Lion Desktop.")

6. If you want to require passwords for the PDF file to be used, click **Security Options**. The PDF Security Options dialog box appears as shown in Figure 7.8.

7. If you want people to have to enter a password to open the PDF file, check the **Require password to open document** check box and type the password in the Password and Verify fields.

8. If you want a password to be required for someone to copy content from the document, check the **Require password to copy text, images and other content** check box and type the password in the Password and Verify fields.

9. If you want a password to be required for the document to be printed, check the **Require password to print** document check box and type the password in the Password and Verify fields.

10. Click **OK**. The dialog box closes and you return to the Save dialog box.

11. Click **Save**. The PDF file is created.

FIGURE 7.8   You can protect a PDF by creating passwords to protect various actions.

> **NOTE: Viewing PDFs**
>
> Mac OS X Lion includes the Preview application, which is its default PDF reader. An overview of Preview is provided in Lesson 4, "Touring Lion's Applications." You can also download the free Adobe Reader from www.adobe.com.

Summary

In this lesson you learned how to install, configure, and use printers. In the next lesson, you learn how to work with mice, trackpads, and keyboards.

LESSON 8

Working with Mice, Keyboards, and Trackpads

In this lesson, you learn how to configure and use mice, keyboards, and trackpads to control your Mac and to provide input to it.

Understanding Input Devices

Until we arrive at the neural interfaces predicted by science fiction, we need physical ways to control and provide input to our Macs. In this lesson, you learn about the three primary input devices with which you are likely to work: mice, keyboards, and trackpads.

There are many types of these devices available from Apple and other manufacturers. The options include different physical controls, such as the number of buttons, and special functions, such as the ability to program the device to perform specific actions at the push of a key. iMacs include Apple's Magic Mouse and Wireless Keyboard, and Mac Pros feature the Magic Mouse and a wired keyboard with the computer. MacBooks and MacBook Pros include built-in keyboards and trackpads. The Mac mini doesn't come with any input devices.

There are other types of input devices that you might use, including tablets that enable you to provide input to your Mac via a pen, headsets that enable you to speak to your Mac, and so on. However, mice, keyboards, and trackpads are the types of input devices you are most likely to use and are the focus of this lesson.

Regardless of the specific device you want to use, there are two general steps to working with input devices:

1. Connect the device to the Mac. There are two basic ways to do this. One is to use a USB cable. The other, and more common way these days, is to use Bluetooth to connect with the device wirelessly. (Of course, you don't need to connect a MacBook's or MacBook Pro's keyboard or trackpad because they are built in, but you might choose to add an external device, such as a mouse, to your mobile Mac.)

2. Configure the device. You use the relevant panes of the System Preferences application to configure the device. For example, you use the Trackpad pane to configure the gestures you want to use on a trackpad.

NOTE: **Old-Fashioned Wireless**

Initially, wireless devices used radio frequencies (RF) to communicate. Although this worked fine, and even had some advantages over Bluetooth, RF required a transmitter that you had to connect to the Mac, which was a nuisance, especially when you used a mobile Mac. Almost all wireless devices use Bluetooth, but if you encounter one of the RF devices, you can use and configure them in similar ways. You just need to take the additional step of connecting the RF transmitter to your Mac.

Working with Mice

At the risk of being pedantic, a *mouse* is a device that you move to cause the pointer to move on the screen and whose buttons you use to take action; the Apple Magic Mouse's top surface also enables you to use gestures to control your Mac as if you were using a trackpad. Many types of mice are available, and they have different features and feel differently in your hand. They also come in a variety of sizes. All current mice share the capability to cause the pointer to move on the screen and have at least two buttons, although most have more than that.

Like other input devices, current mice connect to your Mac with a USB cable or wirelessly.

Connecting to a Wired Mouse

This is kind of an obvious section because connecting a wired mouse is a one-step task (but being a compulsive type, I needed to include it anyway). Connect the mouse's cable to a USB port on your Mac, on its display, or on a USB hub. After the mouse is connected, you're ready to configure and use it.

Connecting to a Bluetooth Mouse

Using a Bluetooth mouse is nice for a couple of reasons. One is that a cable doesn't hinder your mouse movements. Another is that your mouse doesn't tie up a USB port, which is useful for so many things, such as connecting hard drives, iPhones, and so on.

A Bluetooth connection is set up between two devices through a process called *pairing*, where each device recognizes the other and they are paired so that they can communicate with each other. A single device can communicate with more than one other Bluetooth device at the same time. Each device with which your Mac communicates over Bluetooth must be paired separately.

Sometimes pairing requires you to enter a passcode on one or both of the devices being compared, sometimes you just need to review the passcode to make sure it is the correct one, and in other cases, no passcode is involved.

Before you connect a Bluetooth device, make sure Bluetooth is configured on your Mac by performing the following steps:

1. Open the Bluetooth pane of the System Preferences application. The center part of the Bluetooth pane shows the devices with which your Mac is currently communicating or the No Devices message if you haven't paired it with any devices yet (see Figure 8.1).

FIGURE 8.1   This Mac is not paired to any Bluetooth devices—yet.

2. Check the **On** check box. Bluetooth services start.

3. Check the **Discoverable** check box. This makes your Mac discoverable by other devices because your Mac transmits signals that other devices can detect. You can still connect to your configured Bluetooth devices when this box is not selected; your Mac just won't be able to be automatically detected by other devices.

4. Check the **Show Bluetooth status in the menu bar** check box. This places the Bluetooth menu on the menu bar, making it easier to control Bluetooth from the desktop. You are ready to configure a Bluetooth mouse.

NOTE: **Advanced Bluetooth**

If you click the Advanced button on the Bluetooth pane, a sheet opens. On this sheet are additional configuration controls for Bluetooth. These include how your Mac reacts if it doesn't find a keyboard, mouse, or trackpad when it starts up, whether Bluetooth devices can wake your computer, and so on. In most cases, the defaults are fine, but you can also open the sheet to change them if needed.

To connect a Bluetooth mouse to your Mac, you use the Bluetooth Setup Assistant. Follow these steps:

1. Power up the mouse, and if it is not auto-discoverable, which most mice are not, then press its discoverable button. This is usually a small button located on the bottom of the mouse. When you push this button, the mouse goes into Discoverable mode, which causes the device to start broadcasting a Bluetooth signal your Mac can detect. Apple's wireless mice become discoverable when you turn them on (the Magic Mouse has a slider on the bottom side that you use to turn it on); the green light on the bottom of the mouse flashes when it is discoverable.

2. Open the Bluetooth menu and select **Set Up Bluetooth Device** or, if the Bluetooth pane is still open, click **Set Up New Device.** The Bluetooth Setup Assistant opens and searches for Bluetooth devices.

3. Click the **mouse** to select it.

4. Click **Continue.** Your Mac attempts to pair with the device. When the process is complete, the Conclusion screen displays. The Bluetooth mouse is ready to configure.

5. Click **Quit** to close the assistant.

NOTE: **Know When You Are Connected**

You can use the Bluetooth menu's icon to tell whether you are currently connected to a device. If you are connected, the icon changes from a dark Bluetooth symbol to a gray symbol with three dots across it. As you connect or disconnect devices, a graphic icon momentarily appears on the desktop, too. For yet another way, open the Bluetooth pane of the System Preferences application. In the center part of the pane, the current status (such as Connected) of each Bluetooth device with which you've paired your Mac is shown.

Configuring a Mouse

After you have connected a mouse to your Mac, configure its controls. With this mouse, you can provide input using your fingers on the top surface; these motions are called gestures. The following steps are for an Apple Magic Mouse (mice that have other features are configured for those specific features, but the general process is the same):

1. Open the Mouse pane of the System Preferences application, as shown in Figure 8.2.

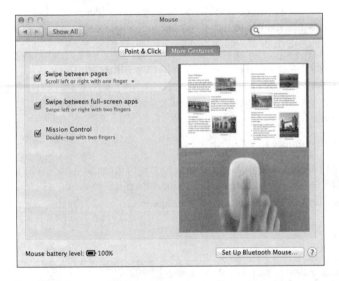

FIGURE 8.2   Use the Mouse pane to configure how a mouse works.

2. Point to the **Scroll with finger direction** gesture so it becomes highlighted in a gray box. A video showing the finger motion and what it does plays in the preview window. These videos help you understand what each gesture does.

3. If you want the content you are viewing, such as a webpage, to move in the same direction as your fingers, check the **Scroll with finger direction** check box. For example, when you browse a webpage and move your fingers toward the top of the mouse (away from the Apple logo), the content of the page moves up the screen. With this check box unchecked, when you move your fingers toward the top of the mouse, the content of the page moves down the screen.

4. Check the **Secondary click** check box to use a gesture to perform a secondary click. Like the other gestures, a video shows you what the gesture is and what it does.

5. If you enabled the secondary click gestures, use its menu to choose **Click on right side** or **Click on left side**.

6. Check the **Smart zoom** check box if you want to be able to zoom by tapping twice with one finger.

7. Use the **Tracking** slider to determine how fast the cursor moves relative to the mouse movement. If you move the slider to the left, the pointer travels a smaller distance across the screen for the same mouse movement.

NOTE: **Mac OS X Lion Scrolling**

If you've used a Mac or another computer before, you may find Mac OS X Lion's scrolling behavior with the check box in step 2 checked a bit confusing because it is opposite of how prior versions of the Mac OS X worked (which is how it works with the box unchecked). Lion scrolling works like an iPhone, iPod, or iPad in that the content moves in the same direction as your finger on the screen; i.e., you pull down the screen to move content down. To me, this isn't quite as natural when using a mouse as it is when you are using your fingers directly on the screen. You might want to try using the mouse with the check box checked and with it unchecked to see which works better for you.

NOTE: **Third-party Hardware**

Support for Apple hardware, such as mice, keyboards, and trackpads, is built in to Mac OS X. For devices from other manufacturers, you might need to install supporting software. Typically, these devices include a software installer on a disc; otherwise, you can download it from the company's website. When you install the device's software, you might see configuration panes for the device in the Other section of the System Preferences application. Use the panes specific to the devices with which you are working to configure those devices instead of Mac OS X's default panes.

Working with Keyboards

Keyboards are used for two purposes: input and control. You use the input function to type and the control function to activate commands, navigate, and so on. Like mice, there are two basic types of keyboards, wired or wireless. Also like mice, keyboards can have many features beyond just the basics. You can choose the keyboard that has the features and comfort level that best suit your preferences.

Connecting to a Wired Keyboard

Connecting a wired keyboard to your Mac is a simple matter of plugging its USB cable into an available port on your Mac, a display, or a USB hub. After that's done, you are ready to configure it.

Connecting to a Bluetooth Keyboard

The steps to connect your Mac to a Bluetooth keyboard are quite similar to those to connect it to a Bluetooth mouse (or any other Bluetooth device, for that matter):

1. If you haven't enabled Bluetooth on your Mac, do so using the first set of steps in "Connecting to a Bluetooth Mouse" earlier in this lesson.

2. Turn on the keyboard and place it in Discoverable mode. Some keyboards have a button that you push. The Apple Wireless Keyboard goes into Discoverable mode when you turn it on.

3. Open the Bluetooth menu and select **Set Up Bluetooth Device.** The Bluetooth Setup Assistant appears and begins scanning for devices.

4. Select the keyboard and click **Continue,** as shown in Figure 8.3.

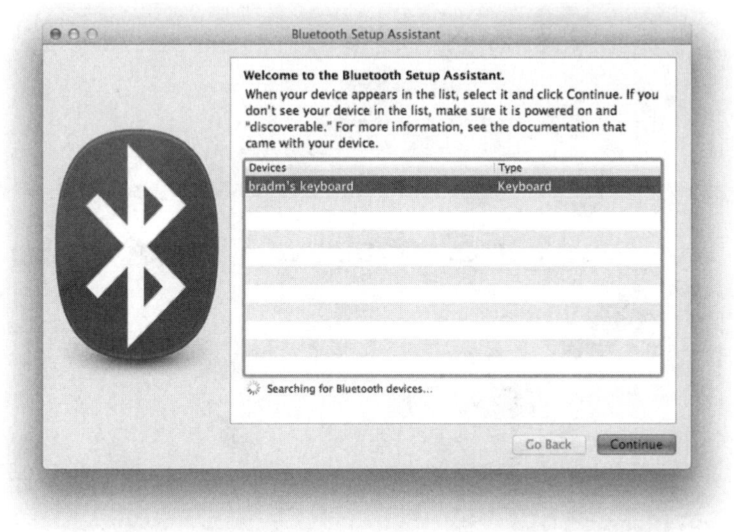

FIGURE 8.3   Choose the keyboard with which you want to connect via Bluetooth.

5. On the keyboard, type the passkey shown in the Assistant window and press Return. If you enter the correct passkey, the Conclusion screen displays, indicating the two devices are paired. The keyboard is ready to configure.

6. Click **Quit**.

Configuring a Keyboard

The following steps show an Apple Wireless Keyboard being configured, but configuring other types of keyboards is similar:

1. Open the Keyboard pane of the System Preferences application.

2. Click the **Keyboard** tab.

3. If you are configuring a MacBook or MacBook Pro's internal keyboard, a USB keyboard, or an Apple Wireless Keyboard, skip to step 5 because you move directly to the configuration screen shown in Figure 8.4.

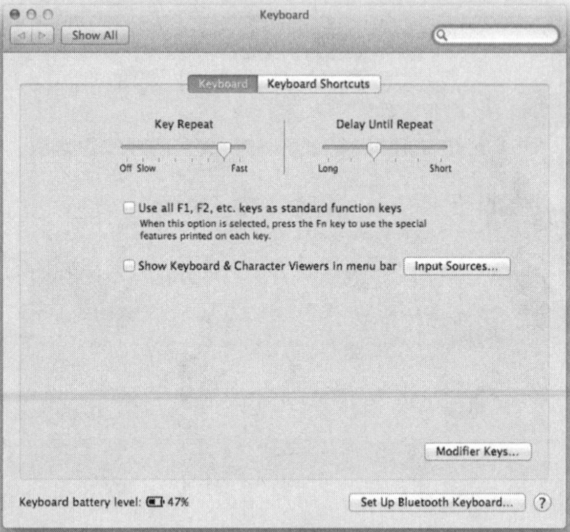

FIGURE 8.4   Use this screen to configure a keyboard.

4. Click the **Set Up Bluetooth Keyboard** button.

5. When the keyboard is found, click **Continue.** You move to the configuration screen for the keyboard.

6. Use the **Key Repeat** slider to set how fast a key repeats when you hold down the key.

7. Use the **Delay Until Repeat** slider to set how much time passes while you are holding down a key until it starts repeating.

8. Check the **Use all F1, F2, etc. keys as standard function keys** check box if you don't want the function keys to perform the

special functions as indicated by their icons and want them to act as regular function keys instead. For example, with the check box unchecked, pressing F4 opens the dashboard; with it checked, pressing F4 activates whatever command is associated with that key in an application.

> TIP: **Alternate Function Keys**
>
> You can activate the "other" function of a function key by holding down the fn key when you press it. For example, if pressing F4 opens the Dashboard, you can press fn+F4 to activate the command associated with the F4 key in an application.

9. If you want the Keyboard & Character Viewers to be shown via the Input menu on the menu bar, check the **Show** check box.

> NOTE: **Keyboard Shortcuts**
>
> Keyboard shortcuts are an important tool in using a Mac more efficiently. For example, instead of opening an application's menu and selecting the Quit command, you can just hold down the cmd key and type Q. Many keyboard shortcuts are ready for you to use; they appear next to the associated commands on menus. You can change default keyboard shortcuts and create your own using the Keyboard Shortcuts tab on the Keyboard pane.

> TIP: **Keyboard Lighting**
>
> MacBook Pro and MacBook Air keyboards have backlit keys. You can use the **Automatically illuminate keyboard in low light** check box to enable this. Then use the slider to determine how long the lighting remains on.

Working with a Trackpad

A trackpad is nice because it stays in one place and only your fingers have to move; plus, it enables you to use all kinds of gestures to control your Mac. If you've used an iPhone, iPod, or iPad, you know how convenient this can be. If you have a MacBook, MacBook Air, or MacBook Pro, a trackpad is built in. If you have another type of Mac, you can add an external trackpad such as Apple's Magic Trackpad that replicates the features of the trackpad in mobile Macs.

NOTE: **Connecting to a Magic Trackpad**

Before you can configure a Magic Trackpad, you must connect it to your Mac. Use the same steps as described for a Bluetooth mouse or keyboard.

To configure a trackpad, use the following steps (which are based on a MacBook Pro's internal trackpad):

1. If you are configuring an external trackpad, power it up and connect it to your Mac.

2. Open the Trackpad pane of the System Preferences application.

3. If you are configuring a mobile Mac's internal trackpad or there is only one Bluetooth trackpad connected to your Mac, skip to step 4 because you move directly to the configuration screen shown in Figure 8.5.

4. If you have more than one Bluetooth trackpad available, click the **Set Up Bluetooth Trackpad** button.

5. When the trackpad is found, click **Continue.** You move to the configuration screen for the trackpad.

   Now configure the gestures you want to use; gestures are motions of your finger on the trackpad. You can use one-finger, two-finger, three-finger, and four-finger gestures to scroll, navigate, and so on.

6. Click the **Point & Click** tab. The gestures for pointing and clicking are shown.

7. Point to a gesture you are interested in using. A video showing the finger motion and what it does plays in the preview window. These videos can help you understand what each gesture does.

8. To enable a gesture, check its check box. For example, if you want to be able to perform a secondary click with a gesture, check the **Secondary click** check box. When you check a box, the associated gesture is enabled.

FIGURE 8.5   You can use the Trackpad pane to determine how your trackpad works, including the gestures you want to use.

9. If the gesture has options, use the pop-up menu to configure them. For example, when you use the secondary click gesture, you can select **Click or tap with two fingers**, **Click in bottom right corner**, or **Click in bottom left corner** to choose the specific gesture you want to use. When you change an option, the gesture's video is updated so it reflects the change you made.

10. Repeat steps 7 through 9 to configure all of the Point & Click gestures.

11. Use the **Tracking Speed** slider to determine how fast the cursor moves relative to your finger movement. If you move the slider to the left, the pointer travels a smaller distance across the screen for the same finger movement.

12. Click the **Scroll & Zoom** tab.

13. Use steps 7 through 9 to configure the gestures you want to use for scrolling and zooming.

14. Click the **More Gestures** tab.

15. Use steps 7 through 9 to configure these gestures, which include working with Mission Control, the Launchpad, and so on.

NOTE: **Mac OS X Lion Scrolling**

If you've used a Mac or other computer before, you may find Mac OS X Lion's scrolling behavior with the check box in step 6 checked a bit confusing because it is opposite of how prior versions of the Mac OS X worked (which is how it works with the box unchecked). Lion scrolling works like an iPhone, iPod, or iPad in that the content moves in the same direction as your finger on the screen; i.e., you pull down the screen to move content down. To me, this isn't quite as natural when using a mouse as it is when you are using your fingers directly on the screen. You might want to try using the mouse with the check box checked and with it unchecked to see which works better for you.

Summary

In this lesson you learned how to use the primary types of input devices, which are mice, keyboards, and trackpads. In the next lesson, you learn how to configure and use Mac OS X Lion user accounts.

LESSON 9

Configuring and Managing User Accounts

In this lesson, you learn how to create and manage user accounts on your Mac. You also learn how to configure the login process and use Fast User Switching.

Understanding User Accounts

Mac OS X Lion is a multiuser operating system, which simply means it is designed to be used by multiple people on the same Mac. Like using other kinds of user accounts, to access a Lion user account, you log in to the software using a username and password. After you're logged in, you have access to the system resources and personalization associated with that user account.

> NOTE: **Never Logged In?**
> It's entirely possible that you've used your Mac without ever entering a username and password. That's because Lion includes the Automatic login feature that logs in to a designated user account automatically. You learn how to enable or disable this feature later in this lesson.

Each Mac OS X user account can include the following:

▶ System preferences, such as Dock configuration, desktop picture, and so on.

▶ Application preferences, such as default fonts, view options, and so on.

▶ Account configurations, including email accounts.

▶ Ability to install applications and configure other aspects of Mac OS X Lion.

▶ Home folder, which is where all the user's documents and personalization are stored.

▶ Restrictions that can include access to only specific applications, system functions, or people (via text chatting or email).

Even if you don't share your Mac with others, you should configure at least one additional user account on it. (As noted, you already created one user account the first time you started up Mac OS X Lion.) In addition to the initial user account, you should create a "clean" account, meaning one under which you don't change any default preferences, that you can use to troubleshoot problems.

Mac OS X includes the following types of user accounts:

▶ **Administrator**. Administrator accounts are the second-most powerful type of user account; when logged in under an Administrator account, you have complete access to the System Preferences application to make changes to the operating system, such as to create and manage user accounts and change network settings. Administrators can also install software that everyone who uses the Mac can access.

> NOTE: **My First User Account**
>
> The first time you started up Mac OS X Lion, you created a user account, though it isn't obvious that is what you are doing. This first user account is an Administrator user account.

▶ **Standard**. Someone logged in under a Standard user account can only make changes related to that specific account. For example, a Standard user can change her desktop picture and application preferences but can't install applications or create other user accounts.

▶ **Managed with Parental Controls**. The Lion Parental Controls feature enables you to limit the access that a user has to various kinds of content, such as email and websites. When you manage this kind of account, you determine specific types of content, applications, and other areas the user can access. People using this type of account are prevented from doing all actions not specifically allowed by their Parental Control settings.

▶ **Sharing Only**. This type of account can only access your Mac to share files across a network and has no access to the operating system or other files that aren't being shared.

▶ **Group**. Access to folders and files on your Mac is determined by each item's Sharing and Permissions settings. One of the ways you can assign privileges to an item is by configuring a group's access to it; a group user account is a collection of user accounts and is used only to set access privileges. You create a group, assign people to it, and then use the group to set access permissions for files and folders.

NOTE: **Root Account**

If you read closely, you might have noticed I called the Administrator user account the second-most powerful kind of account. There is one more type of account, which is called the root account. Mac OS X is based on the UNIX operating system, which is where the root account comes from. The root account is even more powerful than an Administrator account because it has no limits on what you can do while logged in under it. You can delete critical system files, access any system resources, and so on. The root user account is typically only useful when troubleshooting problems. In fact, most Mac OS X Lion users never need to use it, and so its details are not included in this lesson.

Creating User Accounts

You can create as many user accounts of the various types as you'd like. As mentioned previously, you should have at least two Administrator user accounts, which include the account created during the initial startup process and a troubleshooting account.

You can create Administrator, Standard, Managed with Parental Controls, or Sharing Only user accounts by performing the following steps:

1. Open the **Users & Groups** pane of the System preferences application, as shown in Figure 9.1. On the list on the left side of the window are the current user accounts. The user account under which you are logged in appears at the top of the list, and its details appear in the right pane of the window along with the tools you use to configure that account. At the bottom of the user list are the Login Options button, the Add and Remove buttons, and the Action menu.

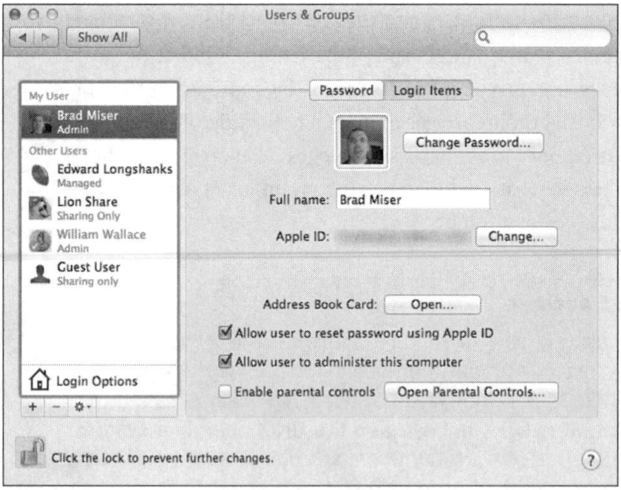

FIGURE 9.1   You administer the user accounts on your Mac using the Users & Groups pane of the System Preferences application.

2. Authenticate yourself if needed.

> NOTE: **Authentication**
>
> Certain changes you make, such as creating user accounts, are limited to Administrator user accounts. Before you can perform these actions, you have to authenticate yourself as an Administrator. You typically do this by clicking a locked "lock" icon, entering an Administrator account's username and password, and

clicking Unlock. You have to do this even if you are already logged in under an Administrator user account.

3. Click the **Add** button. The New Account sheet appears.

4. On the **New Account** pop-up menu, choose the type of account you want to create. For example, pick Standard to create a Standard user account or Administrator to create an Administrator account. The rest of these steps are for a Standard account, but you can use the same basic process to create any type of account.

5. Type a name for the account in the **Full Name** field. This can be just about anything you want, but usually a person's actual name works best.

6. Edit the account name if you want to change it. By default, this name is all the words in the full name combined with no spaces, but you can change it to be something else. This name appears in a number of places, such as in the path to the user's Home folder. It's a good idea to keep the account name short, and you can't include any spaces or special characters in it.

CAUTION: **No Password**

You can leave the password fields empty, and the user account won't have a password. Although this is convenient for the user, it isn't secure. You should usually include a password, and you should always include one for Administrator accounts.

7. Type the user's password in the **Password** and **Verify** fields. You can create any password you'd like; try to include at least eight characters and mix in numbers and letters to boost security.

TIP: **Creating Passwords**

If you want some help creating passwords, click the Key button next to the Password field. The Password Assistant opens; you can use it to create passwords and see their level of security.

8. Type a hint about the password in the **Password hint** box. This hint helps a user log in to his account when he can't remember the password.

9. Click **Create User** as shown in Figure 9.2. The user account is created and appears on the list of accounts. You are ready to customize it by adding an image and configuring other elements.

FIGURE 9.2   This user account is ready to be created.

After you've created a user account, you can immediately configure its other properties, or you can update the account at any time.

An image, such as a photo or other graphic, can be associated with user accounts; user account images appear in various locations, such as the Login window. Mac OS X automatically chooses an image for each user account from the default images it has. You can leave this image as is, or you can use the following steps to customize the user account with an image of your choice:

1. Move to the **Users & Groups** pane of the System Preferences application and authenticate yourself (if needed).

2. On the Accounts list, select the user account with which you want to associate an image.

3. Click the image well, which is the box located to the left of the Change or Reset Password button. (When you select the account currently logged in, the button is Change Password; when you select a different account, the button is Reset Password.) The Edit picture sheet appears. At the top of the sheet is the Edit Picture command. Below that are Lion's default images.

4. To choose one of the default images, select its icon from the pop-up menu and skip to step 8.

5. To use a custom image, click **Edit Picture.** The Edit Picture sheet appears. In the center pane, the current image appears. At the top is a pop-up menu that enables you to select any picture you've recently used. Toward the bottom of the sheet is the size slider, and below that is the button you use to capture a photo with your Mac's camera. At the very bottom are the buttons you use to choose an image from the desktop, cancel the change, or select the picture.

6. To use a photo as the account's picture, position the camera so it captures the photo you want to use and click the **Take photo snapshot** button. The timer activates and, when it expires, the photo is taken; skip to step 8.

7. To use a graphic file on your Mac as the account's picture, click **Choose**, move to and select the image you want to use, and click **Open.** The image you selected is copied into the sheet, as shown in Figure 9.3.

8. Set the portion of the image that is displayed by dragging the slider to the right to include less of the image or to the left to include more of it. The portion of the image that will be displayed is shown within the selection box; the part of the image outside the box and grayed out will not appear.

9. Drag the image inside the box until the part you want to be displayed is contained within the box. You might need to use the slider in conjunction with this step to get the image the way you want it to look.

Recent Pictures

Take photo snapshot

Choose...   Cancel   Set

FIGURE 9.3   I've added this user's image to his account.

10. Click **Set.** The Edit Picture sheet closes, and the image you configured appears in the Image well on the Accounts Users &
Groups pane.

Now configure the following options to complete the setup of the user
account:

▶ If the user has a an Apple ID, click **Set**, type his Apple ID in that
field on the resulting sheet, and click **OK.** This associates the
user's Apple ID account with the Mac OS X user account.

▶ To allow the user to reset his user account password with his
Apple ID, check the **Allow user to reset password using Apple
ID** check box. This adds another way (in addition to using the
hint you configure) for the user to be able to regain access to his
Mac OS X user account should he forget his password.

▶ To allow the user to administer the computers, check the **Allow
user to administer this computer** check box. This changes the
account's type to Administrator.

▶ When you select the account currently logged in, you can click the **Open** button to set the user's Address Book card.

▶ The remaining option enables you to configure Parental Controls for the user account, which is covered in the next section.

NOTE: **Sharing Only**

A Sharing Only user account has the fewest options; you can set its image, apply an Apple ID, or allow the user to reset the password using the Apple ID.

Creating a Group user account is simple:

1. Create the user accounts you want to place into a group.

2. Select Group on the New pop-up menu on the New Group sheet, and enter the group's full name.

3. Click **Create Group.** The sheet closes and the user accounts on your Mac appear in the Membership area.

4. Check the check box for each user you want to place in the group, as shown in Figure 9.4.

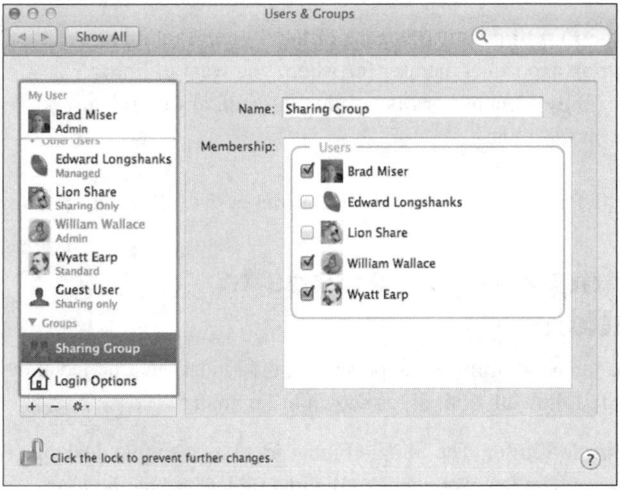

FIGURE 9.4   This group includes the users whose names are checked.

NOTE: **Guest User**

The Guest User account is created automatically. You can use this account to determine whether guests are allowed to log in to your Mac. When a guest logs in, she can access public resources or those you have shared with Everyone. You can also allow or prevent guests from accessing shared folders.

Applying Parental Controls to User Accounts

Parental Controls enable you to limit the access a user has to various areas of Mac OS X Lion and to certain functionality. Although the name of the feature implies it is useful for parents, you can use it for anyone who might benefit from having a simpler user interface and who would benefit from having fewer options. To apply Parental Controls to a user account, use one of the following options:

▶ When you create a new user account, select **Managed with Parental Controls** on the New Account pop-up menu.

▶ Select a user, check the **Enable parental controls** check box, and click **Open Parental Controls**.

▶ Open the **Parental Controls** pane of the System Preferences application and select the user for whom you want to limit access. (Only Standard or Managed with Parental Controls users appear on this pane.)

Each tab of the Parental Controls pane is covered in the following sections.

Restricting a User's Access to Applications

Use the Apps tab to set limits on applications, the Finder, and the Dock by configuring the following options, as shown in Figure 9.5:

▶ **Use Simple Finder.** The Simple Finder presents a simple desktop to the user. The Dock contains only three folders; when the user clicks a folder, it opens on the desktop and the user has access to the applications that you enable and to documents that she creates. Within Finder windows, everything opens with a single click.

FIGURE 9.5   If you don't want a user to be able to access specific applications, use the Apps tab of the Parental Controls pane.

▶ **Limit Applications.** To limit the user's access to applications, check the **Limit Applications** check box and do the following:

    ▶ On the **Allow App Store Apps** pop-up menu, select the age restrictions on the applications downloaded from the Mac App Store; select **All** to allow all apps to be used; select an age, such as **up to 9+**, to limit access to applications based on their age rating; or select **Don't allow** to prevent the user from accessing any apps from the Mac App Store.

▶ On the Allowed Apps list, click the disclosure triangle next to
the application categories to expand or collapse them. Check
the check box next to each application you want the user to be
able to use; conversely, uncheck the check box to prevent the
user from accessing the application.

TIP: **Searching for Apps**

Use the Search tool at the top of the Allowed Apps list to search
for a specific application for which you want to allow or prevent
access.

▶ **Allow User to Modify the Dock.** Check this check box to allow
the user to modify the Dock; uncheck it to make the user use the
Dock as-is.

Restricting Access to the Web

On the Web tab, you can limit the websites the user can visit. To do so, use
the following options:

▶ **Allow unrestricted access to websites**. Select this option to
allow the user to access any website.

▶ **Try to limit access to adult websites automatically**. Select this
option to have Safari prevent access to adult websites. Click
Customize and use the resulting sheet to allow or prevent access
to specific websites (in addition to those limited by the tool
automatically).

▶ **Allow access to only these websites**. Select this option to create
a list of websites the user is able to visit. To add websites to the
list, click the **Add** (+) button, select **Add Bookmark**, enter the
website title and URL, and click **OK**.

TIP: **Adding Folders**

To organize the websites you allow, select **Add Folder** on the Add
pop-up menu and name the folder. Drag websites into a folder to
place them there. Click a folder's disclosure triangle to expand or
collapse its contents.

Restricting Chat and Email

The People tab enables you to designate with whom the user can chat or email. To set these limits, click **People** and do the following:

▶ **Limit Mail**. Check this check box to place limits on people with whom the user can email.

▶ **Limit iChat**. This check box places limits on the people with whom the user can chat.

▶ **Allowed Contacts**. The people on this list determine who and how the user can interact via email or chat. To allow the user to communicate with a person, click the **Add** (+) button. Enter the person's name and email address and select **Email** or **AIM** (to allow email or chatting) on the pop-up menu. Use the **Add** (+) button to add permission for the other option (Email or AIM) if you want to allow both types of communication, as shown in Figure 9.6. Click **Add person to my address book** to add the contact information to your Address Book. Then click **Add.** You return to the Allowed Contacts list and see the permissions you added.

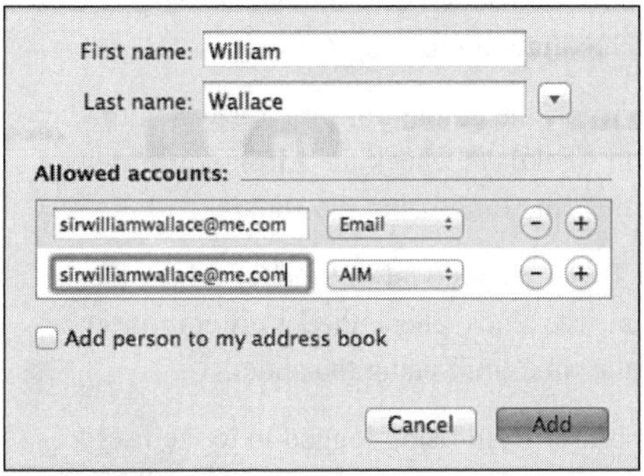

FIGURE 9.6   Use this sheet to allow the user to communicate with a person via email or chat.

TIP: **Adding Contacts from the Address Book**

If you click the expand triangle on the Add Person sheet, you can access your Address Book to use its information to add people to the Allowed Contacts list; if you do this, you don't have to type any contact information.

▶ **Send permissions requests to**. If you check this check box and enter your email address in the box, you receive emails when someone not on the Allowed Contacts list attempts to contact the user. Using these emails, you can allow or prevent communication between the requestor and the user account you are configuring.

CAUTION: **Limits on People**

The People limits work only for Mail and iChat. If you have other email or chat applications, you need to prevent the user from accessing those applications (via the Apps tab) to ensure he can communicate only with the people you designate.

Setting Time Limits

These tools enable you to control how much time and when the user can use the Mac. You have the following options:

▶ **Weekday time limits**. To set the amount of time for which the user can be logged in on weekdays, check the **Limit computer use** check box and set the time limit using the slider.

▶ **Weekend time limits**. To set the amount of time for which the user can be logged in on weekends, check the **Limit computer use** check box and set the time limit using the slider.

▶ **Bedtime**. To prevent the user from being logged in to the user account for specific periods of time Sunday to Thursday, check the **School nights** check box and enter the time period during which user activity should be prevented using the two time boxes. To prevent the user from being logged in to the user account for specific periods of time on Friday and Saturday, check the **Weekend** check box and enter the time period during which user activity should be prevented using the two time boxes.

Controlling Other Actions

The Other tab enables you to configure the following permissions:

▶ **Hide profanity in Dictionary**. With this check box checked, the user won't see any words classified as profane in the Dictionary application.

▶ **Limit printer administration**. With this option checked, the user is unable to add or change printers.

▶ **Limit CD and DVD burning**. Check this check box to prevent the user from being able to burn CDs or DVDs.

▶ **Disable changing the password**. If you don't want the user to be able to reset her password, check this check box.

TIP: **Checking Activity**

You can use the Logs button to open a log showing various kinds of activity the user has been doing. If you are concerned about what a user is up to, use the logs to check it out. You can then use the Parental Controls to further limit access if needed.

Opening Documents and Applications Automatically at Login

This feature causes documents or applications to open automatically when a user logs in to an account. To configure this, you must be logged in as the user you want to configure. Click the **Login Items** tab, and do the following:

▶ **Add applications or documents**. Click the **Add** (+) button, move to and select the items (documents or applications) you want to open automatically, and click **Add.** The items you selected are added to the list and open automatically when the user logs in.

▶ **Remove applications or documents**. To prevent an item from opening automatically, select it and click the **Remove** (-) button.

▶ **Hide items automatically**. If you want an item to open automatically and then be hidden, click its check box. For example, you might want Mail to open but work in the background until you have new email rather than taking up screen space.

Configuring the Login Process

To access a user account, you log in to it using the account's name and password. Initially, Mac OS X Lion is set to automatically log in to the first user account you created. You can turn automatic login off so that you must choose a user account each time you log in. You can configure a number of other aspects of the login process.

To configure the login process, open the Users & Groups pane of the Systems Preferences application and click the Login Options button at the bottom of the user list. The login option controls display in the right side of the pane, as shown in Figure 9.7.

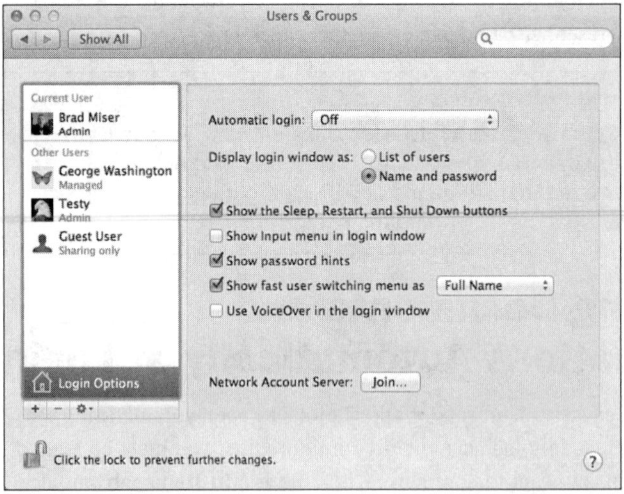

FIGURE 9.7   Configure the Login process using the Login Options tools.

Set the following options:

▶ **Automatic login**. On this pop-up menu, select the user account you want to be logged in automatically each time you start your Mac. You're prompted to enter the password for that account; do so and click **OK.** The next time your Mac starts up, this account is used automatically. To disable automatic login, select **Off**.

▶ **Login window**. Select the **List of users** radio button if you want the Login window to display a list of the user accounts on your

Mac. To log in, the user clicks an account and enters its password. Select **Name and password** if you want empty name and
password fields to appear instead; in this case, the user has to
enter the account name along with the password.

▶ **Show the Sleep, Restart, and Shut Down buttons**. When enabled,
this option presents these three buttons on the Login window.

CAUTION: **Shut Down Button on the Login Window**

If you use Automatic login, disable the Sleep, Restart, and Shut
Down buttons option. If you leave it enabled, someone can access
your Mac by shutting it down and restarting it. Because the login
process happens automatically, a password is not needed. This
makes is simple for anyone to gain access to your Mac without
credentials.

▶ **Show input menu in login window**. Select this option to include
the Input menu on the Login window; this menu enables the user
to select from the keyboard/language options you have configured.

▶ **Show password hints**. Check this to show the password hint
associated with a user account upon a failed login attempt.

▶ **Show fast user switching menu as**. This option controls how the
Fast User Switching (explained in the next section) menu is identified on the Finder menu bar. The options are Long Name, which
shows the current user account's long name at the top of the Fast
User Switching menu; Short Name, which shows the short name;
and Icon, which identifies the menu with a silhouette.

▶ **Use VoiceOver in the login window**. Enable this option to have
VoiceOver speak the text on the Login window to assist sight-
impaired users with the login process.

Working with Fast User Switching

Fast User Switching enables you to quickly change user accounts without
having to log out of one account to log in to another. This is useful because
a user can be left logged in, which means all her application processes can

continue to run. You can switch to a different user account to use that account; then you can switch back to the first account again in the same way. You access Fast User Switching via its menu on the Finder menu bar (in the previous section, you configured how this menu is identified).

Open the menu by clicking the user account full name, user account short name, or silhouette. The Fast User Switching menu appears, as shown in Figure 9.8. Users who are currently logged in are marked with a check mark. The active account is also grayed out.

FIGURE 9.8   The Fast User Switching menu enables you to quickly change user accounts.

To change user accounts, click the account you want to use. The Login window displays with that user account selected. Enter the password and click **Login.** If the account is currently logged in, you pick up right where the user left off; if it wasn't logged in, you log in to the account "from scratch."

TIP: **Quick Security**
To quickly secure your Mac, select Login Window. You remain logged in to your account, but the Login window appears. Your Mac

can't be used without the account's password being protected. It's a good idea to do this whenever you leave your Mac unless it is in a secure location.

To change how the menu is identified, select **Show** and pick the option you want (these are the same as on the Login Options pane).

Select **Users & Groups Preferences** to open the Users & Groups pane of the System Preferences application.

Changing User Accounts

Over time, you might want to change configuration of user accounts, such as to add Parental Controls or to change the user's picture. To do this, open the Users & Groups pane and select the user whose account you want to change. Use the tools that appear to make changes to the account. These work just as when you create an account.

> TIP: **Logged-In Users**
>
> If a user is logged in, his user account is marked with a check mark and is grayed out on the user account list. Before you can make any changes to a logged-in account, you or the user must log out of it.

Deleting User Accounts

If you no longer need a user account, you can delete it by selecting it on the user account list and clicking the **Delete** (-) button. Then choose one of the following options:

▶ **Save the Home folder in a disk image**. All the files in the user's Home folder are saved into a disk image located in the Deleted Users folder under the Users folder. You can access the files in the disk image by opening it.

▶ **Don't change the Home folder**. If you choose this option, the user's Home folder remains in its current location under the user's folder in the Users folder, but its permissions are changed so that you can access it from an Administrator user account.

▶ **Delete the Home folder**. If you choose this option, all traces of the user are removed from the Mac. (To make the deletion even more permanent, select the **Erase home folder securely** check box.)

Click **OK**, and the user account is deleted and the user's Home folder is handled according to the option you selected.

Summary

In this lesson you learned how to create and manage your Mac's user accounts and the login process. In the next lesson, you learn how to secure and protect your Mac and its data.

LESSON 10

Securing and Protecting Your Mac

In this lesson, you learn how to protect your Mac and safeguard its data.

Understanding Threats to Your Mac

The world is a dangerous place; you've likely heard that before, and, unfortunately, there are risks in the digital world as there are in the physical one. There are two general sources of risk: intentional attacks and malfunctions (user, hardware, or software).

Your Mac is designed to be connected—to the Internet and to local networks. These connections bring with them pathways for people to try to cause trouble for you and to do you harm such as by stealing your identity. Fortunately, with a few relatively simple tools and techniques, you can significantly reduce the risk of a successful attack against you and your Mac.

Malfunctions can be user error (and we all make mistakes now and then), hardware problems, software issues, and so on. Although not intentional and not likely to lead to things like identity theft, the effect of malfunctions can be very severe, with things like the loss of irrecoverable photos or financial records and other events that are either costly or impossible to recover from. The good news is that it is also relatively easy to almost eliminate the risk of losing data as long as you take action before the data is lost.

Updating Your Software

Because people are actively trying to come up with new ways to compromise security and because no software or hardware is perfect, software is regularly updated to patch security holes, solve bugs, and make other improvements. Part of protecting your Mac and its data is ensuring that you are using the most recent versions of software. There are two types of software you need to keep current: Apple software and third-party software. How you maintain current software is different for both types.

Updating Apple Software

Because it is the largest factor in how secure your Mac and its data are, Mac OS X is the most important software you need to keep current. Mac OS X's Software Update tool lets you easily keep Mac OS X and your Apple applications current. Although you can update software manually, it's a better idea to configure Software Update so that it checks for and downloads updates automatically. Follow these steps:

1. Open the Software Update pane of the System Preferences application.

2. Click the **Scheduled Check** tab if it isn't selected already.

3. Click the **Check for updates** check box.

4. On the **Check for updates** pop-up menu, select the frequency with which your Mac checks for updates, as shown in Figure 10.1.

5. If you want updates to be downloaded automatically, check the **Download updates automatically** check box. I recommend that you check this check box so updates are downloaded as soon as they are found. If you don't check this check box, you're prompted to download updates when they are available.

6. Quit the System Preferences application.

When the specified amount of time passes, Software Update checks for new software. When it finds new versions, it downloads them automatically and then prompts you to allow them to be installed or prompts you to allow them to be downloaded and then installed (if you didn't check the option explained in step 5). Just follow the onscreen prompts and you'll successfully install the software updates.

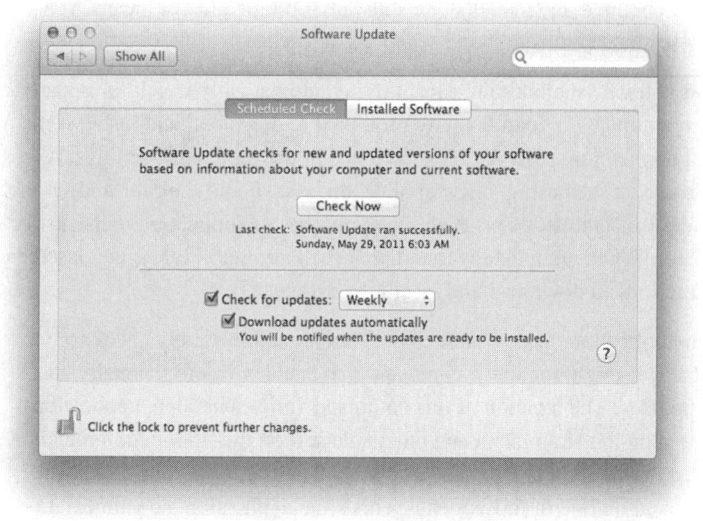

FIGURE 10.1   Configure your Mac to automatically look for and download updates to your Apple software.

TIP: **Updating Manually**

To check for updates manually, click the Check Now button or select Apple menu, Software Update. The Software Update application checks for updates to your Apple software. If some are found, you're prompted to download and install them. Software Update guides you through the process.

Updating Third-party Software

You will also use lots of third-party software (anything not produced by Apple). It's also important to update this software for the same reasons as you should update your Apple software. How you update third-party software depends on how you installed that software.

If you obtained and installed the software through the App Store application, use that application to check for, download, and install updates. This is explained in Lesson 3, "Installing, Using, and Managing Applications."

If you obtained and installed the software through another means, you have several options to identify and install updates.

Most software includes the capability to automatically check for updates; when an update is found, you're prompted to download and install it. In most applications, this option is included in the preference settings. As soon as you start using a new application, you should look for and set this preference. In most cases, each time you start an application it checks for updates. When an update is found, you see a prompt. Follow the onscreen instructions to download and install the update.

If an application doesn't include a feature to automatically check for updates, it might include a command that enables you to manually check for updates. The location of this command varies, but some applications place it on the Help menu and others place it on the *Application* menu, where *Application* is the name of the application. If you don't see this command on one of those menus, check the application's documentation.

After you've selected the command to check for updates, if an update is found, you see onscreen instructions to download and install it.

In some cases, applications don't include any type of check for updates feature, though thankfully almost all do these days. If you can't find a command to check for updates, visit the software developer's website and check for the latest version; visit the Support section to download and install updates.

Protecting Your Mac from Internet Attacks

Connecting to the Internet exposes your Mac to various types of attacks. These can include attempts to steal your identity, to use your Mac to launch other attacks, and so on. You don't really need to worry about the types of attacks you might experience; just know that your Mac can be attacked unless you protect it. Fortunately, you can guard against most attacks using relatively simple tools.

Using a Base Station to Guard Your Mac

To protect your Mac, and the rest of the devices on your local network, you should install and use a base station or hub. This device serves several purposes, especially providing local network services, a connection to the Internet for all the devices on your network, and so on. It can also serve to protect your network from attack.

The best hub choice for most Mac users is an AirPort Extreme Base Station or a Time Capsule because support for administering the AirPort networks they provide is built in to Mac OS X. Also, these base stations shield your network from Internet attacks.

Creating a network is explained in Lesson 6, "Connecting Your Mac to the Internet and a Local Network." However, assuming you are using an AirPort Extreme Base Station or Time Machine, you should double-check to ensure it is configured to protect your network:

1. Open the AirPort Utility application located in the Utilities folder within the Applications folder.

2. Select the base station you want to check.

3. Click **Manual Setup**.

4. If prompted, enter the base station's password and click **OK.** The AirPort Utility moves into Manual mode. In this mode, you can make changes to the base station directly and access all possible settings for it.

5. Click the **Internet** tab.

6. Click the **NAT** sub-tab.

7. Ensure the **Enable NAT Port Mapping Protocol** check box is checked, as shown in Figure 10.2; if it is, skip to step 9.

8. If the **Enable NAT Port Mapping Protocol** check box is not checked, check it.

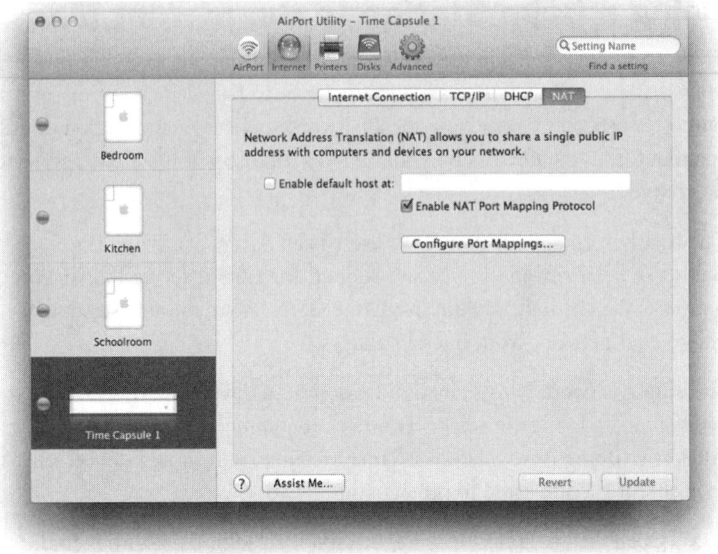

FIGURE 10.2 Using NAT Port Mapping helps guard your network and the devices connected to it from attack.

NOTE: **Network Address Translation**

When Network Address Translation (NAT) is active, the only Internet Protocol (IP) address exposed to the Internet is the base station's. This shields the devices connected to the Internet through the base station from Internet attacks because devices outside your base station cannot identify the devices on the network; they see only the base station, which cannot be hacked like a computer can.

---

9. Click the **AirPort** tab.

10. Click the **Wireless** tab.

11. If the Wireless Security setting is **None**, configure the wireless network to use one of the security options, such as WPA/WPA2 Personal.

NOTE: **Wireless Security**

You should always secure your wireless networks. This requires that someone provide a valid password to be able to join the network. If you don't require this, any device within range of your network can join it and launch attacks against the devices connected to it.

12. If you made any changes, click **Update**; if not, just quit the AirPort Utility application.

Configuring Your Mac's Security and Privacy

Mac OS X includes a number of general security settings that are particularly useful if you use your Mac in a variety of locations, some of which might allow it to be accessed by someone else. To configure these settings, do the following:

1. Open the Security & Privacy pane of the System Preferences application.

2. Click the **General** tab, as shown in Figure 10.3.

3. Use the **Require password after sleep or screen saver begins** check box and drop-down box to enable this feature and select the amount of time the computer is asleep or in screen saver mode before a user must type his account's login password to stop the screen saver or wake up the Mac from sleep.

4. To prevent someone from being able to use your computer just by starting it, check the **Disable automatic login** check box. This prevents a user from being automatically logged in so that in order to use your Mac, someone must know the password for at least one user account.

5. To further restrict a user's ability to change system settings, check the **Require an administrator password to access**

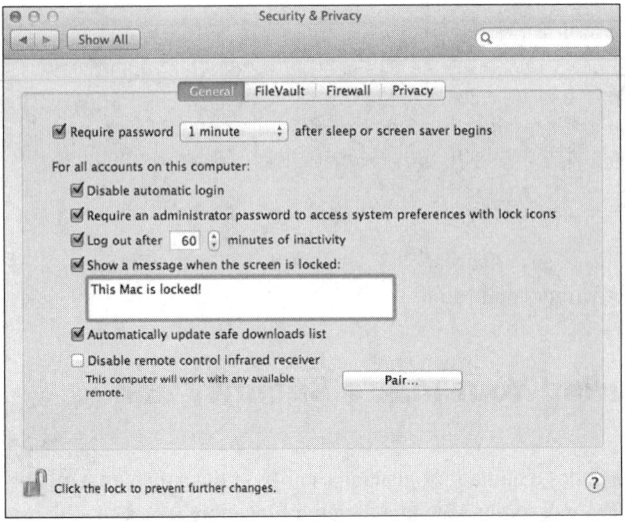

FIGURE 10.3   Use these settings to configure general security preferences.

system preferences with lock icons check box. With this
enabled, you have to authenticate yourself even to see protected
panes.

6. To cause user accounts to be automatically logged out after periods of inactivity, check the **Log out after** check box and set the
amount of inactive time using the time box.

7. To show a message on the screen when the Mac is locked, check
the **Show a message when the screen is locked** check box and
type the message you want to be displayed.

8. To allow your safe downloads list to be updated automatically,
check the **Automatically update safe downloads** list check box.

NOTE: **Safe Downloads List**

The Safe Downloads list is a Mac OS X Security feature intended to
prevent downloading malware and other kinds of software that can
harm your computer. The Mac's Safe Downloads list includes files

---

that are safe to download. You can set Lion to update this list automatically so it has the most current list from Apple.

9. To prevent your Mac from being controlled through an infrared
remote control, check the **Disable remote control infrared
receiver** check box.

10. Click the **Privacy** tab.

11. To prevent data about your Mac from being sent to Apple,
uncheck the **Send diagnostic & usage data** to Apple check box.

12. To prevent applications from accessing location information,
uncheck the **Enable Location Services** check box.

CAUTION: **Disabling Location Services**

If you disabled Location Services, some applications might not
work correctly or some functionality might not work. If you leave
these services enabled, when an application uses them, it is
shown on the application list on the Privacy tab. You can prevent
specific applications from using these services by unchecking their
check boxes.

Using Your Mac's Firewall for Protection

Whenever your Mac isn't protected by a base station or other firewall, be
sure you configure its firewall to protect it from Internet attacks. Common
situations are when you travel and connect to various networks, such as in
public places and hotel rooms. In most cases, these networks are configured to limit access to your computer (similar to how a base station shields
it), but you shouldn't count on this. Instead, protect your Mac with its firewall by performing the following steps:

1. Open the Security & Privacy pane of the System Preferences
application.

2. Click the **Firewall** tab.

3. Click **Start.** The firewall starts running with the default settings.

4. Click the **Advanced** button. The Advanced sheet appears, as shown in Figure 10.4.

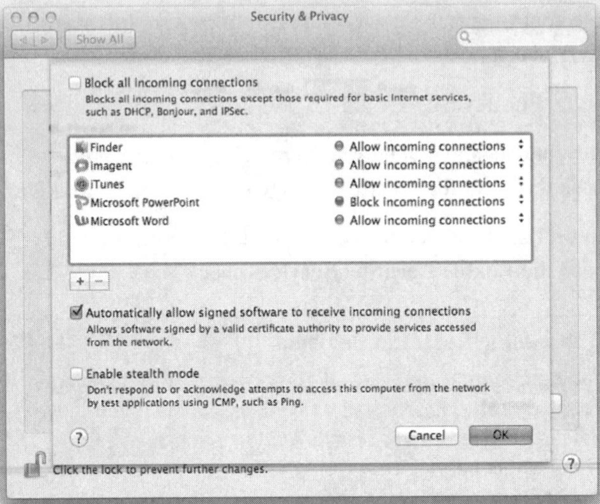

FIGURE 10.4   Use the Advanced sheet to improve the protection the firewall offers to your Mac.

5. To provide the maximum protection, check the **Block all incoming connections** check box. This prevents all connections except those very basic connections required for network access, such as DHCP and Bonjour. If an action you try doesn't work the next time you try it after configuring the firewall, you need to uncheck this check box and perform step 6 instead.

6. Add any applications you are sure you want to allow to have incoming connections or block all incoming connections by clicking the **Add (+)** button below the action list, selecting the application you want to add, and configuring its pop-up menu to Allow incoming connections or Block incoming connections.

Applications that are allowed have a green status, and those that are blocked have a red status. Any blocked applications are unable to receive incoming traffic, and functions associated with receiving communication from outside your Mac are prevented. (When you've not allowed a specific application through the firewall and it tries to communicate, you're prompted to allow or prevent it.)

7. To allow applications that have a valid security certificate to receive incoming connections, check the **Automatically allow signed software to receive incoming connections** check box.

8. Select the **Enable stealth mode** check box. This further protects your Mac by ensuring that uninvited connection requests aren't acknowledged in any form so that the existence of your computer is hidden.

9. Click **OK.** Your settings are saved and the sheet closes. Your Mac is protected by the firewall.

Protecting Your Mac from Viruses

Viruses are also designed to harm you by stealing your identity or causing trouble for you. The difference between viruses and other kinds of attacks is that you usually have to do something to trigger a virus attack, and that something it almost always opening a file or clicking a link.

To guard against viruses, there are two general schools of thought. One is that you can adequately protect yourself from viruses by being very careful about accepting files or clicking links, especially when they come to you via email. The other line of thinking is that you should install and use an antivirus application to protect your Mac against viruses.

Both lines of reasoning are valid, and you can certainly live in both camps.

Some pointers to guard against viruses manually include the following:

▶ Never open a file attachment to an email message unless you are extremely sure of the sender or are expecting the file. If in doubt, contact the sender to verify it. If you have a lot of doubt, delete it.

▶ When dealing with emails and file attachments, consider the skill level and knowledge of the sender. If the sender is a new or inexperienced user, she is much more likely to forward messages containing viruses.

▶ Never click a link in an email message that appears to be requesting information from you unless you are 100% sure of the source. In many cases, criminals forge emails that look like they are from legitimate sources. Any email asking you to verify information for banking or other accounts is almost always an attempt to steal your identity; if you requested some kind of change, such as a password change, links in the resulting emails are probably okay. If you are unsure of a link in an email, don't use it. Get more information about it first. Again, if in doubt, hit delete.

▶ When downloading files from the Internet, make sure you are downloading them from a trustworthy site. Legitimate organizations scan files for viruses before making them available for download.

▶ When you open an application for the first time, Mac OS X informs you and asks you to confirm you want it to open. Don't just blindly click Open. Check the name of the application; if it isn't something you intentionally opened, prevent it from opening.

Protecting yourself from viruses manually can work, but it requires diligence and discipline. For maximum protection, install an antivirus application on your Mac. Antivirus applications monitor activity; when known or suspected virus activity is detected, that action is blocked. Most applications update themselves frequently to attempt to keep up with the ever-increasing number of viruses.

One popular and proven antivirus application is Norton AntiVirus for Mac. To get more information about it, visit http://us.norton.com/macintosh/antivirus/.

Protecting Your Data with Encryption

If you travel with your Mac, the data it contains is vulnerable because your computer can be carried away by other people; even if you use a stationary Mac, it can be stolen. If you store important data on your computer, you can encrypt your data so that it can't be used without an appropriate password. Even if someone is able to mount the hard drive in your Mac, he must have the password to be able to access its data.

The Mac OS X FileVault feature encrypts your disk using a password that you create so that this data can't be accessed without the appropriate password.

To configure FileVault, perform the following steps:

1. Open the Security & Privacy pane of the System Preferences application.

2. Click the **FileVault** tab.

3. Click **Turn On FileVault.** You see a sheet listing all the user accounts on your Mac. Each user's password must be entered for that user to be able to unlock the disk. Users who are able to unlock the disk are marked with a check mark; if a user is not able to unlock the disk, you see the Enable User button next to the user account. The account under which you are working is automatically enabled.

4. Click the **Enable User** button for the user you want to allow to unlock the disk.

CAUTION: **Enabling Users**

If you don't enable a user, he won't be able to access encrypted data on your hard drive, which means he won't be able to use the computer.

---

   5. Enter that user's password and click **OK**.

   6. Repeat steps 4 and 5 until you've enabled all the users whom you want to be able to unlock the disk.

   7. Click **Continue**. You see a sheet containing your recovery key. This key is needed in the event you forget your password. You can use the key yourself to recover data. You can then provide this key to Apple and it will be able to help you recover your data.

> CAUTION: **Recovery Key**
>
> If you don't have this key and forget your password, all your data will be lost.

   8. Record your recovery key, such as by writing it down or taking a screenshot, and store it in a secure location; then click **Continue**.

   9. On the resulting sheet, choose to store the key with Apple by selecting **Store the recovery key with Apple** or elect not to by selecting **Do not store the recovery key with Apple**; then click **Continue**.

   10. If you elected to store the key with Apple, configure your security questions on the resulting sheet and click **Continue**; if not, skip this step.

   11. Click **Restart**. Your Mac restarts.

   12. Log back in to your user account. The encryption process begins.

While the encryption process runs, you may or may not notice anything. The process can take quite a while depending on how much data you have on your Mac. To see the status of the process, open the FileVault pane again, as shown in Figure 10.5. You see that FileVault is turned on, and if you sent a recovery key to Apple, you see a confirmation that it was done. If the process is ongoing, the encryption status bar is shown below that.

If you see an exclamation point icon near the bottom of the pane, as in Figure 10.5, you need to click the Enable Users button and enable each user who appears for them to be able to use the Mac.

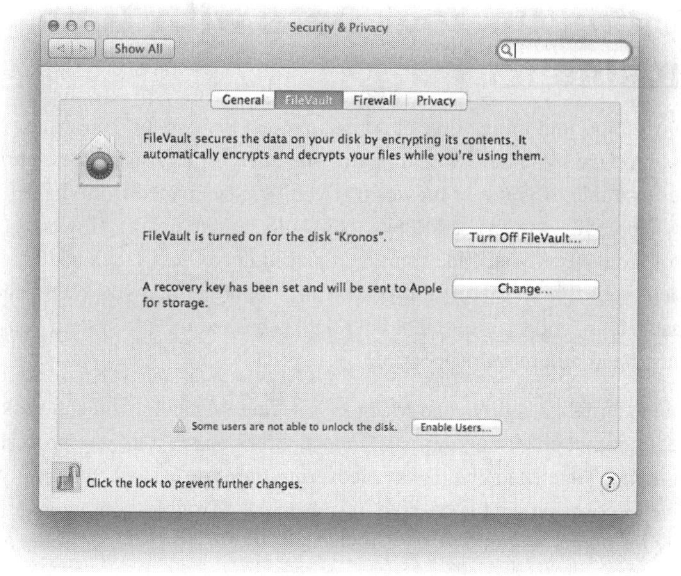

FIGURE 10.5   FileVault encrypts the data on your hard drive.

After the process is complete, you won't notice any difference because data is decrypted as needed when you log in. The difference is when someone tries to access the disk without the password, in which case, all the data on the disk is useless. For example, suppose someone steals your Mac. Although she can't access your user account without your login password, she could connect the computer to a FireWire drive with Mac OS X installed and start up from that volume. Because the files on your Mac's startup volume are not protected anymore (the OS on the computer to which the Mac is connected is running the show), they are accessible. If FileVault is not on, these files are not encrypted and can be used, but if FileVault is on, these files are encrypted and are useless unless the password is known.

Backing Up Your Data with Time Machine

The most important thing you can do is to protect the data on your Mac. Much of the data you have would be time-intensive or expensive to re-create (for example, if you lose movies that you've downloaded from the iTunes Store, you would need to pay to download them again). However, some of the data on your Mac can't be replaced in any way (such as the photos in your iPhoto Library). It is critically important that you keep your data backed up, and to ensure that your data is backed up, the system you use must be as automated as possible.

With an external hard drive and Mac OS X's Time Machine, you can back up with minimal effort on your part; in fact, after you set it up, the process is automatic. Time Machine makes recovering files you've lost easy and intuitive (recovering data is covered in Lesson 11, "Troubleshooting and Solving Problems").

Time Machine backs up your data for as long as it can until the backup hard drive is full. It stores hourly backups for the past 24 hours and stores daily backups for the past month. It stores weekly backups until the backup drive is full. After the drive is full, it deletes the oldest backups to make room for new backups. To protect yourself as long as possible, use the largest hard drive you can and exclude files that you don't need to back up (such as system files for Mac OS X) to save space on the backup drive.

NOTE: **Time Machine without a Hard Drive**

Time Machine also backs up files to your Mac's startup hard drive automatically. This provides some level of protection for your data during those times when your Mac isn't connected to your backup drive. However, if something happens to the startup drive, your back ups can be damaged. So you should not rely on this local backup feature to protect your data.

To use Time Machine, you need to gain access to an external hard drive and then configure Time Machine to use it.

Preparing a Backup Drive

To use Time Machine, you need an external drive on which to store your backed-up data. You can use any of the following options:

▶ **Time Capsule.** This Apple device is a combination AirPort Extreme Base Station and hard drive. With capacity options of 1TB or 2TB, you can gain a lot of backup storage space. Additionally, a Time Capsule is a fully featured AirPort Extreme Base Station, so you can also use it to provide a wireless network. It also makes an ideal backup drive for any computer connected to the AirPort network it provides. The downside of Time Capsule is that it is more expensive than a standard hard drive, but if you don't already have an AirPort Extreme Base Station, it is slightly less expensive than buying the base station and hard drive separately.

▶ **Hard drive connected through USB, FireWire (400 or 800), or ThunderBolt.** You can use a hard drive directly connected to your Mac as a backup drive. This provides the fastest performance of any option, and hard drives are inexpensive and easy to configure.

▶ **Shared hard drive.** You can back up to a hard drive that you can access through File Sharing over a local network.

NOTE: **Connecting a Hard Drive**

The first time you connect a hard drive to your Mac, you are prompted to use it for Time Machine. If you allow this, you don't need to select the drive as described in the next section because it is selected for you automatically. You can still configure the Time Machine as described in that section.

Configuring Time Machine Backups

To configure Time Machine, perform the following steps:

1. Open the Time Machine pane of the System Preferences application.

2. Drag the slider to the **ON** position. Time Machine activates and the selected drive sheet appears (see Figure 10.6).

FIGURE 10.6   Select the disk you want to use to store your data.

3. Select the drive on which you want to store the backed-up information.

4. Click **Use Backup Disk**.

5. If you selected a Time Capsule or another location that is protected by a password, type the password and click **Connect**; if not, you don't need to do anything for this step. The sheet closes and you return to the Time Machine page. The drive you selected is shown at the top of the pane, and the timer starts the backup process, which you see next to the text Next Backup.

CAUTION: **FileVault and Backups**

If you use FileVault to encrypt your data, you also need to encrypt your backups; otherwise, someone who gets access to your backup disk might be able to recover its data. If you want the backed-up data to be encrypted, check the **Encrypt backup disk** check box. This prevents the data from being used without the encryption passcode. If you check this, make sure you never lose the password.

6. Click the **Stop** button next to the text Next Backup. This stops the backup process so that you can configure it more specifically.

7. Click **Options.** The Do not back up sheet appears. This sheet enables you to exclude files from the backup process. For example, you can exclude the System Files and Applications if you have those files stored elsewhere, such as on a DVD.

8. Click the **Add (+)** button. The select sheet appears.

9. Move to and select the folders or files you want to exclude from the backup; then click **Exclude**.

10. If you selected system files, click **Exclude System Folder Only** to exclude only files in the System folder or **Exclude All System Files** to exclude system files no matter where they are stored.

11. If you are using a mobile Mac and don't want the backup process to run when you are operating on battery power, deselect the **Back up while on battery power** check box.

12. If you want to be warned as old backups are removed from the backup drive, check the **Warn after old backups are deleted** check box. This is a good idea because it lets you know when your backup drive fills up.

13. To prevent versions of documents that you have backed up from being overwritten by changes that are automatically saved (explained later in this chapter), check the **Lock document** check box and select the amount of time after which the versions are locked and won't be changed by later versions created with Auto Save.

14. Click **Save.** You return to the Time Machine pane, which displays information about your backup as shown in Figure 10.7.

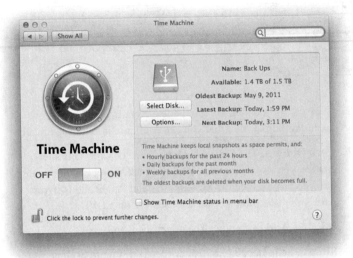

FIGURE 10.7   Select the disk you want to use to store your data.

The timer starts and, when it expires, the first backup is created. From then on, Time Machine automatically backs up your data to the selected hard drive. New backups are created every hour.

15. Select the **Show Time Machine status in menu bar** check box.

To ensure your backup system is working properly, consider the following points:

▶ Every so often, open the Time Machine pane of the System Preferences application and check the status of your backups. This includes the name of the current backup drive, the amount of disk space available, the oldest backup stored on the drive, the latest backup, and the time at which the next backup will be performed. The latest backup date and time tell you how fresh your current backup is; it shouldn't be more than one hour old unless there is a problem, you've disabled Time Machine, or you haven't connected the backup drive to your Mac in a while. If it is more than an hour old, you need to check your system because something isn't working correctly.

▶ As the backup drive gets full, you see warnings when old back-ups are deleted. You need to make sure that there aren't files in the old backups that you might need at some point. This can happen if you delete a document or folder from your Mac but don't restore it for a long time. Eventually, the only copy left might be in the oldest backup that gets deleted when the hard drive gets full.

▶ When your backup system has worked for a while, check the sta-tus of the hard drive you are using. If it is filling up rapidly, con-sider removing some of the system and application files that might be part of it to reduce the space required. The most impor-tant files to protect over a long period of time are those you've created, changed, or purchased. Files that are already on a disc are relatively easy to recover so there's no need to include them in a backup unless the disc is the only place they exist.

▶ If you want to keep certain files but you don't use them anymore, consider moving them onto a DVD or CD for archival purposes. Then delete them from your Mac's hard drive; over time they'll be removed from the backups, or you can exclude them from Time Machine to reduce the amount of drive space required. If the files are important, you should archive them in a couple of ways in case the disc you placed them on is lost or damaged.

▶ Test your backups periodically to ensure things are working properly by attempting to restore some files (explained in the next section). If you don't discover a problem until you need to restore important files, it is too late, so make sure your backup system is working properly. Create a couple of test files for this purpose and let them exist long enough to get into your backups (at least one hour assuming you are connected to your backup drive). Delete some of the files and empty the Trash. Make and save changes to some of the test files. Then try to restore both the deleted files and the original versions of the files you changed. If you are able to restore the files, your data is protected. If not, you have a problem and need to get it solved so that your data isn't at risk.

▶ Use the Time Machine menu on the Finder menu bar to quickly access commands and information. At the top of the menu is the date and time of the most recent backup. You can use the Back Up Now command to start a backup at any time. Select Enter Time Machine to restore files. Select Open Time Machine preferences to move to the Time Machine pane of the System Preferences application.

> TIP: **Online Backups**
>
> You shouldn't rely on one type of backup because each type has a potential for failure (for example, the hard drive you use for Time Machine could stop working and you might be unable to recover). Consider also backing up to DVD or to an online backup system such as www.carbonite.com.

Summary

In this lesson you learned how to protect your Mac and its data. In the next lesson, you learn how to troubleshoot and solve problems.

Troubleshooting and Solving Problems

In this lesson, you learn how to troubleshoot and solve problems.

Solving Problems

Even though Mac OS X Lion is extremely reliable and well matched to the Macintosh computer hardware on which it runs, it is likely that you will encounter some type of problem at some point. In most cases, a few simple steps will correct a problem. In others, you might need to run a utility application to solve a problem. In the most severe cases (which aren't likely to happen because you use a Mac), you might need to restore your Mac from a backup or reinstall Mac OS X.

The most important part of troubleshooting and solving a problem is to remain calm, which is easier said than done (is anything not easier said than done?). Problems seem to happen when you can least afford them, such as when you are neck-deep in a project, and that can lead to frustration. Frustration can lead to inefficient troubleshooting and result in taking actions that actually make the problem worse.

Another important part of troubleshooting is to adopt a logical, step-by-step approach that begins with easy, quick things to try and gets to more complicated tasks if the simpler options don't work. In other words, escalate to more drastic actions only if less drastic actions don't work.

Further, we all need help from time to time, especially when it comes to troubleshooting. Fortunately, the Web is likely to have a solution for (or at least information about) any problem you encounter. If you can't find a solution to a problem via the Web, you can always ask for help; in doing so, make sure you can describe your problem accurately and as completely as possible to increase the chance someone can help you.

Realize there are two general sources of a Mac problem. The most common cause is some sort of software issue, such as a bug or poorly designed feature, user error, and so on. The other potential source of problems is failed hardware.

You can troubleshoot and solve most software problems, which is a good thing because this is far and away the most likely source of problems you might encounter. Accordingly, this lesson focuses on helping you solve software problems.

Hardware problems tend to be quite rare, especially when you are dealing with Apple hardware, which is the good news. They are also most likely to occur soon after you start using something new, which is more good news because the solution is usually covered by a warranty. Unfortunately, hardware problems also tend to be severe, which is not-so-good news. Unless you have the skills and expertise required to solve hardware problems, in almost all cases, you need to take the hardware to experts who can fix it for you, such as Apple repair specialists.

As long as your Mac starts up, you can try to solve its problems using the information in this lesson. If this process fails or a hardware problem prevents your Mac from working at all, you probably need to take your Mac into the shop for repair.

> NOTE: **More Macs Are Good**
>
> In an ideal world, you have another Mac you can use to help troubleshoot problems; this can be yours or someone else's. Having a different Mac enables you to work a problem independently from the Mac that is giving you a hard time. It's even better if you can finish a project you have to get done on the other Mac and then come back to troubleshooting yours later when there is less pressure.

Performing General Troubleshooting Steps

When you encounter a problem, there are several easy and quick things you can do to try to solve it. These simple tasks take care of a whole host of the problems you are most likely to encounter. They should almost always be the first things you try when a problem happens. If they don't work, you must take more drastic action.

Restarting

It's amazing how many problems simply restarting your Mac can solve. Because there's no downside to restarting, it should be one of the first, if not the very first, things you try.

Before you restart, as a precaution, save all your open documents to ensure you have the most recent changes saved. On the **Apple** menu, select **Restart.** At the prompt, check the **Reopen windows when logging back in** check box if you want to pick up right where you are leaving off when the Mac restarts. Click **Restart.** Your Mac restarts; if you selected the Reopen windows option, all your open windows return to how they were when you restarted.

Are you sure you want to restart your computer now?

If you do nothing, the computer will restart automatically in 52 seconds.

☑ Reopen windows when logging back in

Cancel   Restart

FIGURE 11.1   Restarting your Mac is a good first troubleshooting step.

If the problem you were trying to solve is gone, you're done. If not, you have to try another option.

Forcing Applications to Quit

Occasionally, an application hangs, meaning it stops working. The typical symptoms are a frozen screen and the spinning, multicolored wheel that indicates activity without you seeing any results. When an application is hung, you can force it to quit. The primary purpose of this is to enable you to save any work you have in other open applications so you can restart your Mac without losing your work.

CAUTION: **Losing Data**

Forcing an application to quit can cause any data you've created since the last time you saved a document to be lost. To minimize the risk of losing data, don't force an application to quit prematurely; let it exist in the hung state for a few minutes to make sure it won't come back on its own before you pull the plug.

To force an application to quit, open the **Apple** menu and select **Force Quit** or press Option+cmd+Esc. The Force Quit Applications dialog box displays, as shown in Figure 11.2. The name of each application that is hung is shown in red, and its status is indicated next to its name; the names of applications that are running normally are shown in black. (Note: There aren't any hung applications in the figure.)

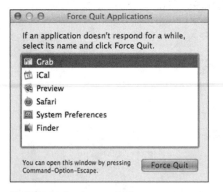

FIGURE 11.2   Use this dialog box to force an application to quit.

Click the application you want to force to quit to select it, and click **Force Quit.** If you are sure you want to do this, click **Force Quit** at the prompt; if not, click **Cancel** instead. The application you selected is shut down; you might or might not lose any unsaved changes in the application's open documents, which is why you don't want to do this unless you are sure the application is hung. Close the Force Quit Applications dialog box.

NOTE: **Relaunch Finder**

Because the Finder application is always running when your Mac is, it can't be quit. However, the Finder can occasionally become hung.

> In this case, select the Finder on the list of applications and click Relaunch. The Finder restarts. If you are able to save all your open documents, do so and restart your Mac.

Now move into each of the other running applications, save any open documents, and quit the application. When you are sure you've saved all your work, restart your Mac.

> CAUTION: **Wrong Keyboard Shortcut**
>
> On the Apple menu, the Force Quit command has the keyboard shortcut Option+cmd+Power. If you press Control+cmd+Power instead, your Mac restarts without allowing you to save changes in open documents. Avoid this keyboard shortcut unless you are sure that's what you want to do.

Shutting Down and Starting Up

Very rarely, your Mac might become hung and stops responding to any commands. If this happens, wait a few minutes to make sure it isn't a temporary situation. If all seems lost, you have to force the Mac itself to quit. This is bad because there is a very good chance (near certainty, in fact) that you will lose all changes in opened documents when you do this. So, you don't want to do this unless it is your only option. When you're sure your Mac is not responding, and it doesn't appear it will anytime soon, press and hold the Power button until the Mac shuts off. Restart your Mac.

Hopefully, any lock-ups are individual events. If your Mac locks up again, you need to solve the problem using one of the techniques discussed later in this lesson.

Checking for Updates

One of the most common problems you'll encounter is bugs in software. Bugs can cause applications to stop working or not work at all, act strangely, or do anything else that seems off.

The only solution for a true bug is to start using an update to the application in which the bug has been removed. If an application you use is behaving poorly, check for an update to it; if one is available, download and install it. Hopefully, the problem is gone after the updated application is in play. Updating software is covered later in this lesson and also in Lesson 3, "Installing, Using, and Managing Applications."

NOTE: **Network Problems**

Information about troubleshooting and solving network and Internet connection problems is provided in Lesson 6, "Connecting Your Mac to the Internet and a Local Network."

Logging In to an Alternative User Account

In Lesson 9, "Configuring and Managing User Accounts," I recommend you create a troubleshooting user account. This is useful because some problems are limited to a specific user account. Being able to access a user account other than the one you typically use is a good way to localize a problem to a specific user account or to determine that it is a more general problem. And, if something happens so your primary user account becomes unusable, you need another account to be able to log in to your Mac.

If you have a problem and the previous solutions don't help, try logging in to your troubleshooting user account. If the problem doesn't recur, you know the issue is related to your user account; this makes it much easier to solve if you need to get help because you can more clearly identify the source of the trouble. If the problem does recur, you know it is general to your Mac.

Starting from the Recovery Partition

Mac OS X Lion includes a Recovery HD volume you can use to start your Mac when the primary system fails. This volume enables you to solve problems with the system software that you can't solve while you are started up from the primary system or in the event that you can't even start your Mac because something has gone wrong with your primary system software.

NOTE: **Alternative Startup Disk**

Previous versions of Mac OS X did not include the Recovery HD volume. You had to use the Mac OS X software install disc to start a

Mac from an alternative drive, or you had to install a version of Mac OS X on a different hard drive than what your primary system was installed on. You can still choose to install Mac OS X Lion on a different disk and use that to run your Mac while you solve problems, but it is more complicated and requires a drive with sufficient space to store the operating system. The benefit is that should your Mac have a problem that prevents the Recovery HD volume from working, you can still run your Mac.

To access the Recovery HD, restart your Mac and then choose to start up from the Recovery HD volume. When you do this, you are able to use the Mac OS X Utilities tool to solve some of the minor and more serious problems you might encounter.

To start up and use the Recovery HD, perform the following steps:

1. If you can shut down your Mac normally, do so; if not, hold the power button until the Mac shuts off.

2. Restart the Mac while holding down the Option key. After a moment, each volume you can use to start your Mac appears. You see at least two options: one is your primary startup volume and the other is the Recovery HD volume.

3. Click the **Recovery HD** volume and press **Return**. Your Mac starts up from this volume. The first screen that appears is the Language Selection screen.

4. Select the language you want to use and press **Return**. The Mac OS X Utilities dialog box appears.

5. Select the utility you want to use to try to solve the problem you are having. The options are

   Restore from Time Machine Backup. Select this option to restore your Mac from your Time Machine backup.

   Reinstall Mac OS X. This option reinstalls the operating system software. If you can't solve the problem in other ways, this option should solve most problems (it won't help if you have a hardware problem). However, it can also remove customizations and configurations you've done and can take a long time, so you shouldn't use this option lightly.

Get Help Online. This option enables you to access the Internet to find help with a problem.

Disk Utility. This option opens the Disk Utility application to try to solve disk or permission issues that may be causing the problem.

NOTE: **More Information**

You can find more information about each of the options in the Mac OS X Utilities in later sections of this lesson.

TIP: **Connecting to the Internet**

To get online help, your Mac must be able to connect to the Internet. When you select the Get Online Help option, you can use the Wi-Fi menu to choose a network to connect to if your Mac isn't connected to an Ethernet network. You need to select a network to connect to because the one you were using might not be selected automatically.

6. After you've selected the option you want to use, click **Continue** and use the resulting tools to implement the solution you are trying. For example, if you select the Disk Utility option, select your primary startup volume and click Repair Disk to try to solve the problem. If you've decided that you need to reinstall Mac OS X Lion, use the install assistant to reinstall the system software.

CAUTION: **Reinstalling Mac OS X**

Be cautious about using this option. Although it often solves even severe problems, in many cases, it requires you to start over with your Mac, such as reconfiguring preferences, re-creating user accounts, and so on. After the reinstall is complete, you also need to run Software Update to ensure you are using the current version of Mac OS X.

To return to your primary system software, restart the Mac and hold down the Option key. This time, select the startup volume instead of the Recovery HD volume.

Repairing Drives with Disk Utility

The Disk Utility application enables you to perform many tasks related to hard drives and other storage devices. For the purposes of troubleshooting and solving problems, you can try to repair the hard drive on which your primary system lives or to repair the permissions on the drive. Either process involves a fair amount of complicated technical information, but you don't need to understand it to be able to use the tool. Run the tool; if the problem is solved, all is well. If not, you have to try other solutions:

1. Restart using the Recovery HD and access the Mac OS X Utilities tool as described in the previous section.

2. Select the **Disk Utility** option. The Disk Utility application opens. Along the left pane are all the volumes mounted on your Mac, as shown in Figure 11.3. The drive at the top of the list is the one on which the active system software is stored. At least two icons for this drive appear; one is for the hard drive itself, which is named with the model and size of the drive, and the other is for the startup volume on which the software is stored, which is named Macintosh HD unless you have changed the name to something else. Another way to differentiate them is that the volume icon is indented under the hard disk icon.

3. Click the **startup volume's** icon.

4. If it isn't selected already, click the **First Aid** tab. The disk and permission repair tools are shown in the right pane of the window.

5. Click the **Repair Disk** button. The application starts checking the disk for problems with the disk's data structure; as it works, progress information appears in the large pane. As problems with the disk are found, the application tries to fix them. You can read along with this information as the tool works; keep your eyes open for any problems that are found but not fixed. When the

process is complete, the overall results are shown. If problems were found and fixed, the problem you were trying to fix might be solved. If problems were found but the application was not able to fix them, you need to try another solution, which might include using a different disk maintenance application or taking the Mac in for repair.

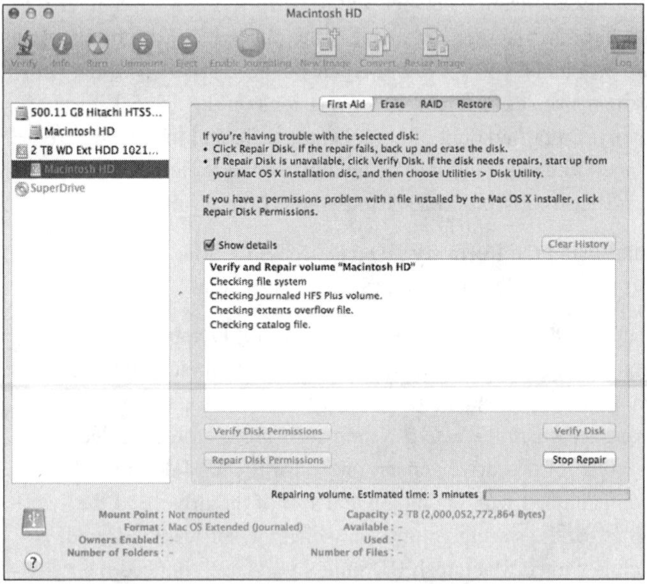

FIGURE 11.3 The Disk Utility application can solve problems with hard disks and disk permissions.

NOTE: **Repair or Verify?**

You'll notice Verify buttons that appear along with the Repair buttons. If you click Verify, the application checks the selected disk for problems but only reports them to you instead of fixing them. Is there any reason to do this? Not really. Just try to repair the disk or permissions and don't bother verifying them first.

6. Click the **Repair Disk Permissions** button. This time, the application checks the permissions applied to the files on the disk and attempts to correct any problems it finds. Like disk repair, information about the progress of the process is displayed in the window. Be alert for any problems found but not solved.

7. When you've repaired the disk and its permissions, quit the Disk Utility application.

   Restart your Mac on the primary startup drive. Hopefully, the problems you were having are corrected. If not, you have to try another solution.

Like the other solutions in this section, repairing a disk and its permissions is easy and really doesn't have a downside, so this is a good thing to try when you are troubleshooting a problem. When you try this, you see lots of technical lingo in the window, but as I mentioned previously, you don't need to worry about what it all means. Take a simplified approach; you don't need to worry about the details of what the application does to be able to solve problems with it.

NOTE: **Disk Utility**

Disk Utility is an application stored in the Utilities folder within the Applications folder. You can run it from the desktop, just like other applications. It works just like it does from within the Recovery HD's Mac OS X Utilities tool, with one big exception. When you run the application from the desktop, it can't repair the hard drive on which the active operating system is installed. So, if you are having a problem with your primary startup disk, start up from the Recovery HD volume and run the application from the Mac OS X Utilities. If you want to work on disk drives you aren't currently using as the startup drive, such as to prepare a new drive for use to repair a drive you are using, run Disk Utility from the desktop.

Recovering Data from a Time Machine Backup

If there is one thing you take away from this book, I hope it is the need to keep your data backed up. Some of the data on your computer, such as photos, simply can't be re-created. Other data is difficult, expensive, or time consuming to re-create. Losing data should be the thing you worry most about when it comes to your Mac. For information about using Time Machine to back up your Mac, refer to Lesson 10, "Securing and Protecting Your Mac."

If you run into a problem where data is lost or you want to replace the current version with a previous version and you have a current backup, you can restore your data from the backup using the Time Machine application.

You can use Time Machine to restore data from within the Mac OS X Utilities tool or from the desktop. Running it from either location is similar. If the only problem you have is the data loss (in other words, your Mac is working fine), you can run it from the desktop. If you've encountered a more serious problem, you might need to run it after starting up from the Recovery HD volume.

You can recover data with Time Machine in two possible ways. One is to access previous versions of your desktop to restore files. The other is to access previous versions of data within an application; most applications don't support this option, but some very important ones (such as iPhoto) do.

To restore data on the desktop with Time Machine, perform the following steps:

1. Open a Finder window showing the location where the files you want to recover were stored. This can be the location where files that have been deleted were placed, or it might be where the current versions of files are stored (in the event you want to go back to a previous version of a file).

2. Launch Time Machine by clicking its icon on the Dock, opening the Time Machine menu, and selecting **Enter Time Machine** or by opening the Launchpad and clicking **Time Machine.** The Time Machine interface replaces the desktop, as shown in Figure

11.4. In the center of the window is the Finder window you opened in step 1. Behind it all the versions of that window that are stored in your backup appear, from the current version to as far back in time as the backups go.

Along the right side of the window is the timeline for your back-ups, starting with today and moving back in time as you move up the screen. Each backup is represented by a horizontal line on the timeline. Some are identified with a label, such as Latest Backup, Today, and so on. Backups in magenta are stored on the hard drive you configured for Time Machine. Backups in gray are stored on the Mac's startup drive. At the bottom of the screen the Time Machine toolbar is displayed. In the center of the toolbar, the time of the window that is currently in the foreground appears. At each end are controls that you use to exit Time Machine (Cancel) and the Restore button (which is active only when you have selected a file or folder that can be restored).

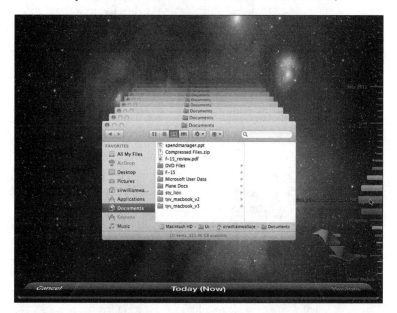

FIGURE 11.4 Time Machine is aptly named because it enables you to go back in time to recover files that are lost.

3. Locate the versions of the files you want to restore by doing any of the following:

Click a time on the timeline when the files you want to restore were available. As you point to a backup, its line is magnified and you see the date and time at which the backup was created.

Click the back arrow (pointing away from you) located just to the left of the timeline. You move back in time and the window as it is captured in the backup is shown.

Click a Finder window behind the foremost one. The window on which you clicked moves to the front; as you move into windows toward the "back" of the stack, you move back in time.

4. When you reach the files you want to restore, select them.

5. Click **Restore.** The files and folders you selected are returned to their locations in the condition they were in the version of the backup you selected, and Time Machine quits. You move back to the Finder's location where the restored files were saved, and you can resume using them.

To use Time Machine to restore data from within an application, perform the following steps:

1. Open the application from which the data was lost. For example, if photos are missing from your iPhoto Library, open that application.

2. Launch Time Machine by clicking its icon on the Dock, opening the Time Machine menu, and selecting **Enter Time Machine** or by opening the Launchpad and clicking **Time Machine.** The Time Machine interface replaces the application window. In the center of the window is the Finder window you opened in step 1. Behind it all the versions of that window that are stored in your backup appear, from the current version to as far back in time as the backups go. This version of Time Machine works just like the one when you are backing up files from the Finder; for example, backups stored on the startup volume are indicated by gray lines and magenta lines indicate backups stored on the Time Machine drive.

3. Locate the versions of the files you want to restore by doing any of the following:

   Click a time on the timeline when the files you want to restore were available.

   Click the back arrow (pointing away from you) located just to the left of the timeline.

   Click a Finder window behind the foremost one.

4. Use the application's controls to move to the photos you want to restore.

5. Select the files, such as photos, you want to restore.

6. Click **Restore.** The files are returned to the application, and you can use them as if they'd never been lost.

NOTE: **Online Backups**

You can also use an online service (such as Carbonite or Mozy) to back up your Mac. The most significant benefit of this approach is that your data is not connected to your Mac in any way, so it is more protected than it is even with Time Machine. For example, if something really bad happens to your Mac, such as a fire or flood, you might lose all the data on it and all the data on your Time Machine drive if it is stored in the same location, in which case you have a real problem. If you use an online backup service, your data remains safe even in an extreme situation like these. You can restore your data to the Mac from whence it came or to a different one.

Reinstalling Mac OS X Lion

Reinstalling Mac OS X is about the most severe action you can take to correct a problem. It is unlikely you will need to do this, but once in a while, it is what you need to do. Here's how:

1. Restart using the Recovery HD and access the Mac OS X Utilities tool as described in the previous section.

2. Select the **Reinstall Mac OS X** option.

3. Click **Continue**.

4. Click **Continue.** This step sends the serial number of your Mac to Apple.

5. Follow the on-screen instructions to complete the re-installation.

Getting Help with Problems

If none of the measures described in this lesson so far have solved a problem, you need to get some help with it. The good news is that a lot of help is available on the Internet and from other sources. There are two basic ways to get help. You can search for help, or you can ask for help.

Searching for Help

Searching for help is the option to try first because you can often find a solution more quickly and easily than by asking for help because you don't need to provide any information to search for solutions. Performing a search is simple.

NOTE: **Mac or Application Help**

Don't forget to try the Mac's or an application's Help system. Open the Help menu and search for help with the problem you are having, or open the documentation associated with the application you are using.

One of the best ways to search for help is to open a web browser and, using your preferred search engine, simply search for the problem you are having. Use a search term that describes the problem you are having; more specific search terms tend to provide better results. In most cases, the results include many links to information about the specific problem you are having, or at least similar problems, as shown in Figure 11.5. Explore the links and try the solutions you find.

FIGURE 11.5 Searching for help is fast and easy and often results in useful information.

If you want to make your search more specific, you can start at sites that are dedicated to Macintosh computers, such as www.apple.com/support, or those specific to software or hardware that you are having trouble with. Most sites offer support areas that enable you to search for problems, read forums, and so on.

Asking for Help

If a search doesn't reveal solutions, you can ask for help with a problem. The most productive places to ask for help are the manufacturers of the hardware or software with which you are having an issue. Typically, their websites contain a support area that enables you to contact customer support.

However, before you ask for help, you need to make sure you are able to ask for help effectively. You should be able to describe the problem you are having with some amount of detail. Otherwise, the person whom you are asking will probably not be able to help or will have to ask you questions to be able to help.

For example, an ineffective question would be something like, "Word quit. Please help." Such messages provide no information that someone can use to help you solve a problem. At worst, an insufficiently detailed request might simply be ignored. At best, you get a reply in which you are asked to provide information that you should have provided with your inquiry.

When you ask for help, provide as much context and detail about the problem as you can. This should include the version of Mac OS X you are using; the versions of the applications that are giving you trouble; and what, specifically, you were doing when the problem happened. The more information you provide, the more likely it is that the person whom you are contacting will be able to offer help. Going back to the prior example, a more effective question might be something like, "I'm running MS Word 2011 with Mac OS v 10.7.1 on a MacBook Pro. When I open the File menu and choose Print, the print dialog box appears briefly, but then Word quits."

If a specific error message appears on the screen when you have a problem, capturing a screenshot can make a request for help much more effective. For example, you can capture the screenshot and attach it to an email request for help.

To capture a screenshot, perform the following steps:

1. With the error message on the screen, open the Launchpad and click **Utilities**.

2. Click **Grab.** The Grab application opens. Because the application doesn't have any windows when you first open it, the only change you'll notice is in the menu bar.

3. Press Shift+cmd+Z, which is the keyboard shortcut for the Timed Screen option. The Time Screen Grab dialog box displays.

4. Click **Start Timer.** The 10-second timer starts.

5. Move back to the error message.

6. Wait for the timer to expire; when it does, the screen is captured and you hear the shutter sound. The screen capture opens in the Grab application.

7. Move into the Grab application.

8. Save the screenshot file. You can provide the file to someone you want to get help from.

> **NOTE: Contact Me for Help**
> Feel free to email me at bradmiser@me.com for help. I'll respond to your request as soon as I am able to.

Summary

In this lesson you learned how to troubleshoot and solve problems. In the next lesson, you learn how to run Windows applications on your Mac.

LESSON 12

Running Windows on Your Mac

In this lesson, you learn how to run Windows applications on your Mac.

Understanding Options to Run Windows on a Mac

Although some of us prefer Macintosh computers, the fact is that a lot more people use Windows computers, especially in businesses and other large organizations. This means that more applications are available for Windows computers, and sometimes an application you have to run is only available for Windows computers. The good news for Mac users is that with Mac OS X Lion, you can run the Windows OS and the Mac OS on the same computer, getting the best of both worlds.

There are two ways you can run the Windows OS and applications on a Mac: Boot Camp and virtualization.

Boot Camp is the Apple technology that transforms Mac hardware into a fully capable Windows PC. You can choose to boot up your Mac in the Mac OS or in Windows. When you boot up in Windows, your Mac becomes a fully functional Windows PC.

The strengths of Boot Camp include great performance (your Mac can out-perform many laptops designed to run Windows only), maximum compatibility for hardware and software, and a lower cost because your only expense is a copy of Windows. A minor downside is that sharing data between the two operating systems can be a bit more complicated because they can't be running at the same time. You also have to restart your computer to switch between the operating systems.

Under virtualization, an application provides a virtual environment (also called a virtual machine) in which you install and run Windows. You install the virtualization application and then install a version of Windows in a virtual machine. When you want to run Windows, you launch the virtualization application, and within its windows you run Windows and Windows applications.

Using a virtual approach has a number of benefits, including being able to run Windows and the Mac OS at the same time because the virtualization software is just another application running on your Mac, good performance (it isn't usually noticeably slower than running it under Boot Camp), and easy data sharing because the Mac OS and Windows are running at the same time.

Virtualization does have two points against it. One is the cost of the virtualization software. The other is that a virtual approach might not be compatible with all the hardware and software you want to run.

Although I've described these as two options, if you chose a virtualization application, you can use both options and switch between them easily.

To run Windows on a Mac, you have to purchase a full copy of Windows 7 to install, whether you use Boot Camp or a virtualization application (or both); you can't use an upgrade (unless of course, you've previously installed a version of Windows on your Mac). The cost for this varies, depending on the version of Windows you purchase and how you purchase it. When you purchase Windows, try to get a version that is designed for builders, also called the original equipment manufacturers (OEM) version. This version is significantly less expensive than the full retail version and is ideal for installing Windows on a Mac.

There are various types of Windows 7, such as Home, Professional, and other categories between which the differences are somewhat difficult to understand. For most Mac users running Windows as a second operating system, the Home version is likely to be sufficient. However, you should compare the versions to make sure one doesn't offer something you need to have; see http://windows.microsoft.com/en-US/windows7/products/ compare for Microsoft's explanations of the differences.

After you have a copy of Windows 7, you're ready to install it. I recommend that you configure Boot Camp even if you end up using virtualization. This gives you the option of running Windows in Boot Camp and, after you obtain and install a virtualization program, under a virtual machine as well.

Installing and Using Boot Camp to Run Windows

Installing and using Boot Camp involves two steps: configuring Boot Camp and then installing Windows. After these steps are complete, you can run Windows on your Mac.

Configuring Boot Camp

Mac OS X Lion includes the Boot Camp Assistant application that guides you through the installation of Windows on your Mac. Here are the steps to prepare your Mac to receive Windows:

1. Open the Boot Camp Assistant application located in the Utilities folder in the Applications folder. You see the first screen of the assistant.

2. Click **Continue.** You see the Download Windows Support Software screen.

3. Click **Download the Windows support software for this Mac**.

4. Click **Continue.** The Assistant downloads the software to your Mac. When the process is complete, the Save Windows Support Software screen displays.

5. Click **Burn a copy to CD or DVD**, insert a blank disc into your Mac, and click **Continue.** The Assistant looks for the drive.

6. When the disc is found, click **Burn.** The software is written to the disc. When the process is complete, the disc is ejected and you're prompted to authenticate yourself.

7. Type your administrator password and click **Add Helper.** The Create a Partition for Windows screen appears. On the left is the partition for Mac OS X, while on the right the partition for Windows, which is a minimum of 20GB, is shown.

8. Set the size of the Windows partition by dragging the Resize handle (the dot) between the two partitions to the left to increase the size of the Windows partition, as shown in Figure 12.1. You can set the partition to be any size you want, but you have to trade off disk space for Windows versus what is available for the Mac OS. I recommend that you allocate at least 50GB to Windows, but if you plan to install a lot of Windows applications and create large documents, you might need a larger partition.

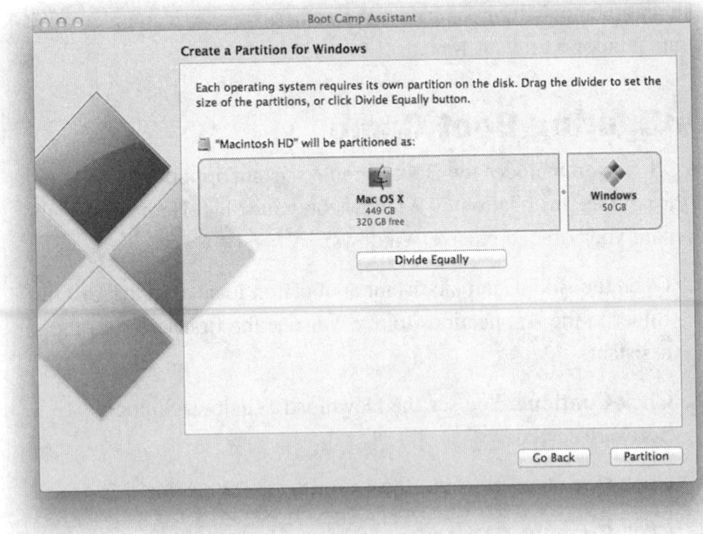

FIGURE 12.1   When you partition your drive, be careful because you don't get a second chance at it without extra time and effort.

CAUTION: **Partitioning for Windows**

When you are partitioning your drive, you can choose to divide its space equally. I don't recommend you do this unless you think you will be using Windows as much as you will the Mac. Also, after you've partitioned your drive, you won't be able to make the Windows partition larger without repartitioning the volume and reinstalling Windows, which is a time-consuming process. So, make sure you give the Windows environment plenty of space.

> NOTE: **More on Partitions**
>
> If the drive on which you are running the Bootcamp Assistant has more than one partition, the assistant won't be able to create a partition for Windows.

9. Click **Partition.** The Assistant creates the Windows partition on your Mac's hard drive.

10. At the prompt, enter your Administrator password and click **Modify Settings.** When the process is complete, you're prompted to insert your Windows installation disc. You are ready to install Windows.

Installing Windows in Boot Camp

Starting from the Insert Windows installation disc prompt, complete the installation of Windows with the following steps:

1. Insert the Windows installation disc.

2. After it is mounted on your Mac, click **Start Installation**.

3. Enter your Administrator password and click **Modify Settings.** The Mac restarts and boots from the Windows installation disc. The installation application starts installing files; the progress is displayed at the bottom of the blue Windows Setup screen. The Windows Starting message appears as the Windows Installer opens.

4. At the prompt, select the language, time and currency format, and keyboard method; then click **Next**.

5. Click **Install Now.** The Setup process begins.

6. Accept the license and click **Next**.

7. Select the **new installation** option.

CAUTION: **Boot Camp Partition Please**

Make sure you select the Boot Camp partition you created earlier to install Windows on. If you don't, you might overwrite a partition with Mac OS X or your data on it, in which case that data is lost.

8. Select the **BOOTCAMP partition.** If an error message appears stating that Windows can't be installed on the selected partition, you need to format the partition by performing steps 9 and 10; if this doesn't appear, skip to step 11.

9. Click **Format.** A warning about files that might be installed on the partition pops up.

10. Click **OK**.

11. Click **Next.** The installation process begins on the partition you selected. Progress information is displayed in the Install Windows window and in the status bars at the bottom of the window. The install process can take quite a while, and your Mac might restart multiple times. Eventually, the Set Up Windows screen appears.

12. Work through the various screens of the Setup Windows application to configure Windows. For example, you need to create a username and password, type the Windows product key, choose how Windows handles updates, and set the time and date. When the process is complete, the Windows desktop appears.

13. Eject the Windows installation disc.

14. Insert the Support Software disc you created earlier.

15. Click **Run setup.exe** and click **Yes** to allow it to install software in Windows. The Bootcamp Installer application opens.

16. Follow the onscreen instructions to complete the installation of various drivers and other software that Windows needs to work with the Mac hardware. You might be prompted to configure various Windows options, such as choosing a network location, while the Bootcamp Installer runs. You can either minimize those until the Bootcamp Installer process is complete or just let the

Bootcamp Installer run in the background and configure Windows while it runs.

17. When the Bootcamp Installer is complete, click **Finish**.

18. Click **Yes** at the prompt to restart your Mac. It starts up in Windows.

Windows is ready to use, but you should update it to ensure you are running the current version by performing the following steps:

1. Log in to your Windows account by typing your password and pressing **Return**.

2. Open the Windows menu, select **Control Panel**, and click the **System and Security** option.

3. Click **Windows Update**.

4. Click **Check for updates**.

5. Follow the onscreen instructions to install all the available updates.

To return to the Mac OS, do the following:

1. To return to the Mac OS, select **Windows** menu and click **Shut down**.

2. Restart the Mac and hold down the Option key while it starts up.

3. Click the **Mac OS X startup disk** and press the **Return** key. The Mac starts up under Mac OS X again.

NOTE: **Back Where You Started?**

When Mac OS X restarts, you might return to the Bootcamp Assistant because Mac OS X restores open windows by default. Because you've already completed the assistant, just quit it.

Using Boot Camp to Run Windows

After you install Windows, you can transform your Mac into a Windows PC by restarting the Mac and holding down the Option key while it starts up. When the available startup disks appear, click the Windows startup volume and press the Return key. The Mac starts up under Windows and you can run your Windows applications.

TIP: **Choosing Windows as Your Default OS**

If you want Windows to be your default OS, open the Startup Disk pane of the System Preferences application and click BOOTCAMP Windows startup disk. Then click Restart again at the prompt. Each time you start your Mac, it opens Windows. You can pick the Mac OS instead by holding down the Option key while it restarts.

TIP: **Choosing the Mac OS as Your Default OS**

To set the default OS to be the Mac OS, start up in the Mac OS and use the steps in the previous tips, except instead of clicking on the BOOTCAMP Windows startup disk, select your Mac startup disk.

To switch back to the Mac OS, use the same process, except instead of clicking on the Windows startup disk, click your Mac OS startup disk.

CAUTION: **Windows Security**

Windows is constantly under attack from viruses, Trojan horses, and other nasty attempts to steal or damage data. Running Windows on a Mac doesn't protect you from these threats when you are using the Windows environment; it's as susceptible to the same attacks that Windows running on PC hardware is. You should install and use security software (such as a good antivirus application) under Windows as soon as you get your Windows environment running, especially if you're accessing the Internet under Windows.

As you run Windows, be aware that you must activate a copy of Windows to keep it running for more than 30 days. When you do this, the copy of Windows you run is registered to the specific computer on which you activate it as a means to limit illegal copies of Windows. Don't activate your copy of Windows until you've used it for long enough to ensure that you've got it configured the way you want and can run it under Boot

Camp, in a virtual environment, or both. Once activated, if you make a significant change, there's a chance you'll have to reactivate it, in which case you'll have to pay for a new copy of Windows to activate it under a different scheme or try to explain the situation to Microsoft to get the previous activation "undone" so you can activate it under a different environment. Running a "nonactivated" version of Windows doesn't limit you in any way, although you do get annoying reminders that it needs to be activated along the way. After you hit the 30-day mark, you have to activate it to continue using Windows.

Installing and Using a Virtual Environment to Run Windows

When you use a virtual environment to run Windows, you don't have to choose one OS or the other because you can run them both at the same time. This makes sharing data between the two environments easy. If you find yourself running Windows often, I recommend you use a virtual approach because it makes switching between Windows and the Mac OS so much easier. And you can do tasks in both at the same time.

There are two primary virtualization programs available: VMware Fusion and Parallels Desktop for Mac. Both of these applications work well and offer a similar feature set. Each also offers a free trial so you can check them out to see which you prefer.

Information about Parallels Desktop for Mac is available at http://www. parallels.com/.

The rest of this section focuses on VMware Fusion simply because that is the one the company I work for has selected; either works well.

NOTE: **Pick an Environment, But Not Just Any Environment**

With either program, you have the option of creating a new Windows environment or using a Windows environment in Boot Camp. I recommend you choose the Boot Camp option because it saves a lot of time installing Windows again in a different environment and might avoid some of the activation issues that can occur

if you run Windows in two different environments. The rest of this
section is based on this approach.

Installing and Configuring a Virtual Environment

To download and install VMware Fusion, perform the following steps:

1. Navigate to http://www.vmware.com/products/fusion/overview.
   html.

2. Click the **Try for Free** button.

3. Create a VMware account by following the onscreen instructions.
   You need to follow an activation process to be able to download
   the application.

4. Download VMware Fusion.

5. When the download process is complete, move back to the desktop and run the Install VMware Fusion application, as shown in
   Figure 12.2.

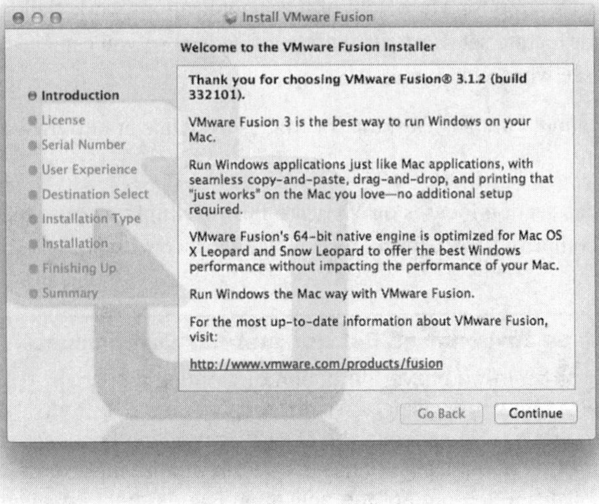

FIGURE 12.2   The VMware Fusion Installer makes setting up the application
straightforward.

6. Follow the onscreen instructions to complete the installation. When the process is done, the completion screen appears.

7. Click **Close** to quit the installer. You're ready to launch VMware Fusion and configure a virtual environment.

Using a Virtual Environment to Run Windows

VMware Fusion automatically detects and uses a Boot Camp installation of Windows so there's no additional configuration. To run Windows, follow these steps:

1. Launch VMware Fusion. The application launches and the Bootcamp environment that has been selected displays.

2. Click the **Start Up** button. The first time you start Windows, some additional preparation has to be done, but for subsequent times, the process is much faster. The first time you should also install the VMware Fusion tools. The VMware Tools Installer launches automatically and begins the installation process. When it is complete, click **Restart** to restart the Windows environment.

3. If prompted to, type your Mac OS X username and password and click **OK.** Windows starts up in the VMware Fusion window.

You're running Windows as shown in Figure 12.3 (Full Screen) and Figure 12.4 (Single Window).

As you run Windows on your Mac, keep these tidbits in mind:

▶ You can move from the Windows OS to the Mac OS by pressing ctrl+cmd, by clicking in an application's window, by selecting it on the Dock, and via all the other standard ways of switching between applications.

▶ You can use the Unity mode so that the Fusion window disappears and all that is shown on the Mac desktop is the VMware Fusion menu on the menu bar and any Windows applications you are running. To try this, select View, Unity when a VMware Fusion application is active. You then access Windows applications by opening the VMware Fusion menu on the menu bar and

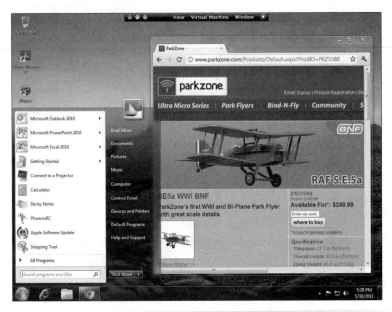

FIGURE 12.3   Is this Windows or a Mac? The answer is yes.

navigating to and selecting the application you want to run. It appears in a new window on your Mac's desktop.

▶ You can copy files from Windows to the Mac or vice versa by dragging them from one environment to the other.

▶ You can also copy information from one environment to the other with the standard copy and paste commands.

▶ Only one environment can be using a CD, a DVD, or another device at the same time. When you insert a disc or connect a device, you are prompted to choose the OS that should use the disc or device. If you've inserted a CD or DVD or connected another device but don't see it on the Mac desktop, the odds are that Windows is running and the disc or device is mounted there, which makes it unavailable to the Mac. Stop the Windows environment; the disc or device appears on the Mac desktop.

▶ You can view the Windows OS in Full Screen mode to have it fill the screen and hide the Mac OS. In this mode, the VMware Fusion toolbar appears at the top of the screen. To change the

FIGURE 12.4   This is VMware Fusion's Single Window mode.

view, open its View menu. Even in Full Screen you can move into the Mac OS as needed. The Full Screen Windows environment moves into the background.

▶ If you have two displays, you can run the Mac OS on one display and have the Windows environment fill the other by running VMware Fusion in Full Screen mode. To try this, run Windows in the Single Window view and then drag the window onto a display. Click the Full Screen button. The Windows environment fills that display, and each OS has its own display.

When you are done running Windows, shut it down by selecting the Windows menu and then clicking Shut down. After Windows shuts down, you can quit the VMware Fusion application.

Summary

In this lesson you learned how to run Windows applications on your Mac.

Index

FREE Online Edition

Your purchase of **Sams Teach Yourself Mac OS X Lion in 10 Minutes** includes access to a free online edition for 45 days through the Safari Books Online subscription service. Nearly every Sams book is available online through Safari Books Online, along with more than 5,000 other technical books and videos from publishers such as Addison-Wesley Professional, Cisco Press, Exam Cram, IBM Press, O'Reilly, Prentice Hall, and Que.

SAFARI BOOKS ONLINE allows you to search for a specific answer, cut and paste code, download chapters, and stay current with emerging technologies.

Activate your FREE Online Edition at www.informit.com/safarifree

> **STEP 1:** Enter the coupon code: MMQCWFA.

> **STEP 2:** New Safari users, complete the brief registration form. Safari subscribers, just log in.

If you have difficulty registering on Safari or accessing the online edition, please e-mail customer-service@safaribooksonline.com

4518053